PRAISE FOR *WHAT IF JESUS WAS SERIOUS ABOUT THE CHURCH?*

The most common word for church in the Ne̶̶̶̶̶̶̶̶̶̶̶̶̶̶̶̶
It's not building or institution or enterprise ̶̶̶̶̶̶̶
church is two words: brothers and sisters. In̶̶̶̶
and me into siblings in a new family. Skye Je̶̶̶̶̶
point chapters in this book sketch a way no̶̶̶̶̶̶
church transformation from the ground up. ̶̶̶̶̶̶̶̶̶
the family God and each of us as brothers an̶̶̶
has been lost in churches that have gotten lost in their vision of church as
corporation and managed by entrepreneurs. The old vision is that church is a
family where Jesus and the Table are the focus. A wonderful book!

SCOT MCKNIGHT, Professor of New Testament, Northern Seminary; author of *A Church Called Tov*

With his characteristic wisdom, insight, and wit, in *What If Jesus Was Serious about the Church?* Skye challenges what church has become in our day and reminds us Jesus intended for His church to be a family. We cannot afford to ignore the issues raised in this book, because our witness, and a generation, are at stake. This is not for the faint of heart, but it is for those who truly care about the church. I was simultaneously challenged and inspired, I know you will be too.

CHRISTINE CAINE, author; founder, A21 and Propel Women

At a time when many are questioning the value of church or giving up on it altogether, Skye Jethani offers a delightful reminder of what church is and is not. Equal parts winsome and wise, this slim primer packs a wealth of biblical insight and offers a compelling vision for what the church of Christ can be.

KRISTIN KOBES DU MEZ, author of *Jesus and John Wayne*

Skye is able to say a lot without using a lot of words. In *What If Jesus Was Serious about the Church*, he is clear, compelling, challenging, and Christ-exalting. After you read this book, you will love Jesus and His church more.

DERWIN L. GRAY, Cofounder and Lead Elder-Pastor of Transformation Church; author of *How to Heal the Racial Divide: What the Bible Says, What the First Christians Knew, about Racial Reconciliation*

We have all had the experience of rebooting our computers when they became cluttered, overloaded, and dysfunctional. What if we could literally reboot the church? In this time of de-churching, deconstructing, politicization, and division, what if we could recapture the passion, energy, and unity of the very first Christians? In this very important book, Skye Jethani shows us how we can.

RICHARD STEARNS, President Emeritus of World Vision US; author of *Lead Like It Matters To God* and *The Hole in Our Gospel*

This book was a breath of theological and practical fresh air! Too often, books about the church tell the same old, stale tale of instructions—go to church; tithe; listen to the sermon; be submitted; don't ask questions. But these dusty formulas often ignore the ancient, powerful, and risky path that God's people were called to undertake—to turn the world upside down by following the wild Jesus into a subversive way of living. Skye Jethani has written one of the most important books about the church I've ever read that every Christian would be wise to read.

A.J. SWOBODA, assistant professor of Bible, theology, and World Christianity at Bushnell University; author of *After Doubt*

Because I love Jesus' church, I thoroughly enjoyed reading Skye Jethani's insights about its importance and beauty. What I particularly appreciated was his emphasis on table spirituality—something our churches desperately need to rediscover. Imagine how the current toxicity of the church could be salved with conversation, bread-and-wine fellowship, and conviviality, particularly among those we disagree with. This book is uncomfortable in necessary ways, but it also serves as a winsome invitation to what we're all longing for the church to become.

MARY DEMUTH, author of *The Most Misunderstood Women of the Bible: What Their Stories Teach Us about Thriving*

If you love the church but sense that we have an identity problem, this book is for you. Skye Jethani's provocative, scripturally centered teachings combined with his vivid drawings will inspire you to be part of the solution. You and I have never needed this book more than now.

KARA POWELL, Chief of Leadership Formation at Fuller Seminary and coauthor of *3 Big Questions That Change Every Teenager*

Our thinking about church is often conditioned on our experience, so we need something that surprises or startles us out of our expectations to think about what Scripture says in a fresh way. *What If Jesus Was Serious about the Church?* does exactly that, by using captivating images and insightful writing to help us evaluate our assumptions about church. This is a resource that critiques and laments our perversions of church—not for the sake of critique, but in order to encourage all Christians to understand and experience the better reality God desires for us.

KAITLYN SCHIESS, author of *The Liturgy of Politics*

What if we have misunderstood the nature of church services, family life, worship, and leadership? With characteristic insight, humor, and relatability, Skye challenges us to reconsider what Jesus said about the church. Moving beyond clichés, Skye provides a profound vision of what it means to be a member of Christ's body. Allow him to challenge your understanding about what Jesus said. You won't regret it.

KYLE STROBEL, coauthor of *The Way of the Dragon or the Way of the Lamb: Searching for Jesus' Path of Power in a Church That Has Abandoned It*

Skye has become my go-to thinker for understanding US politics, church, and evangelical subculture. This book brings together both a challenging critique of today's church and a hopeful vision of the world-changing movement it can be when we take the words of Jesus seriously. I wish a copy could be placed in the hands of every church pastor, home group leader, and congregant out there.

JUSTIN BRIERLEY, presenter of the *Unbelievable?* and *Ask NT Wright Anything* podcasts

A VISUAL
GUIDE TO THE
SPIRITUAL
PRACTICE MOST
OF US GET
WRONG

WHAT IF
JESUS WAS
SERIOUS

ABOUT THE CHURCH?

SKYE JETHANI

MOODY PUBLISHERS

CHICAGO

Some content in this book was previously published on the author's blog or email devotionals. Portions of chapter 22 were first published in "Coming Down the Mountain,"*Leadership Journal* (Summer 2012); portions of chapter 30 were first published in "The Silence Between Notes," ChristianityToday.com, April 29, 2014; portions of chapter 42 were first published in "The Age of DisIncarnation," *Leadership Journal* (Summer 2015); portions of Chapter 47 were first published in "The Platform Principle," *Leadership Journal* (Summer 2011). Used by permission.

The illustration for chapter 47 was adapted from Skye Jethani, *What If Jesus Was Serious?: A Visual Guide to the Teachings of Jesus We Love to Ignore* (Chicago: Moody, 2020).

Edited by Kevin Mungons
Interior and cover design: Erik M. Peterson
Interior and cover illustrations: Skye Jethani

ISBN: 978-0-8024-2427-3

Originally delivered by fleets of horse-drawn wagons, the affordable paperbacks from D. L. Moody's publishing house resourced the church and served everyday people. Now, after more than 125 years of publishing and ministry, Moody Publishers' mission remains the same—even if our delivery systems have changed a bit. For more information on other books (and resources) created from a biblical perspective, go to www.moodypublishers.com or write to:

Moody Publishers
820 N. LaSalle Boulevard
Chicago, IL 60610

1 3 5 7 9 10 8 6 4 2

Printed in the United States of America

For
Mr. Brian Baird
Pastor Cheryl Baird
Dr. Scottie May
Pastor Mary Ellen Slefinger
Mr. Tom Slefinger
Pastor Kathy Woods

"Do not give up meeting together . . .
but encourage one another—and all the more
as you see the Day approaching."

CONTENTS

Introduction

RESTORING FAMILY VALUES

CORPORATIONS NOW STRUCTURE virtually every part of our lives. Born from the ideals of free market capitalism and designed to thrive in a consumer society, these massive companies feed us, clothe us, educate us, entertain us, heal us, and increasingly, some would argue, they even govern us. Few doubt the dominance and effectiveness of corporations. For that reason, over the last fifty years, churches—both large and small—have increasingly copied the values and strategies of corporations as well.

Most of us are probably too young to remember a church prior to the influence of corporate values, but there was a time when most churches weren't program-focused, professionally led institutions with mission statements and HR departments. Throughout most of Christian history, for example, pastors spent most of their time ministering out in the community. They brought the presence of Christ to where their people lived and worked throughout the week—homes, fields, factories, hospitals. Today, corporate values have reversed this pastoral model. Most pastors now stay inside church facilities all week managing programs, and ministry happens when people come to them.

Corporate values have also changed our definition of a faithful church. Corporations are financially and legally compelled by self-interest. Success is measured by the growth of the institution itself, not how it benefits a community or even its industry. Starbucks doesn't just want you to drink coffee; it wants you to drink *Starbucks* coffee. Converting the world from internal combustion to electric vehicles won't make Tesla successful. Convincing the world to buy Tesla's vehicles will. Likewise, we now assume a successful church is a large church. Institutional expansion has gone from a by-product of God's mission to its central goal. This explains why there were only ten megachurches in the US in 1970 (defined as a congregation with 2,000 or more attenders each week), and today there are approximately 1,750.[1]

This emphasis on institutional church growth has even changed our language. Earlier generations spoke about *Christians* and *non-Christians*, or *believers* and *nonbelievers*. But in the era of the church-as-corporation, we now talk about the *churched* and the *unchurched*. These invented words reveal a shift in our missional goal. It's no longer to connect a person with Christ; we want them connected to *our* ministry. The assumption that the church ought to be structured, managed, and measured like a corporation is so widely accepted today that few can imagine anything else.

And yet, Richard Halverson, the former chaplain of the United States Senate, reminds us that the church began as something very different. Long before celebrity pastors, smoke machines, or foyer coffee bars, the church was simply a family:

"In the beginning the church was a fellowship of men and

women centered on the living Christ. Then the church moved to Greece, where it became a philosophy. Then it moved to Rome, where it became an institution. Next, it moved to Europe, where it became a culture. And, finally, it moved to America, where it became an enterprise."[2]

Yes, Halverson oversimplifies two thousand years of history, but his observation remains useful. Indeed, in America the church has become a corporate enterprise. But in its pursuit of expansion, influence, and power, has the church lost the essential Christian values of faith, hope, and love? In its desire to efficiently reach more people and grow as an institution, has it lost its original purpose to make disciples who grow into maturity?

While American corporations are undeniably successful institutions, it's naive to assume their values can be blindly transplanted from the marketplace into ministry and remain equally successful. After all, corporations might generate profits for their shareholders, but they don't have a good track record for generating spiritual health or human flourishing. According to the International Labor Organization, Americans work more, retire later, and take less vacation than workers in any other industrialized country. We are also among the most physically and mentally unhealthy—factors that manifest in higher divorce rates, shorter life expectancy, and other social ills.[3] Likewise, few expect corporations to be pillars of morality or champions of the common good. And never mind the impact of corporations on creation. If this is the fruit of American corporate culture, should we expect the fruit of churches that copy corporate values to be any different?

What we're seeing in the church today—pastoral burnout

and immorality, abuse and cover-ups, financial impropriety, toxic leadership cultures, and the elevation of effectiveness over faithfulness—matches what we've come to expect from giant businesses. It also explains why the age of the corporate church has not only added *churched* and *unchurched* to our Christian vocabulary, it has also given us a new word—*dechurched*. Some church members now feel more like replaceable cogs in a ministry machine rather than essential members of the body of Christ.

As I travel the country to speak, or when I hear from listeners of our podcast, I am amazed by how many have walked away from their churches or are seriously considering it. Very few cite theological or doctrinal disagreements, and some reference recent political upheaval or issues related to the COVID-19 pandemic. Most, however, express a frustration with the corporate machinery of the church—the institutional upkeep, systems, programs, and a general fatigue over the dehumanizing cultures they foster. As one exhausted middle-aged woman said to me, "Is this really what Jesus intended the church to be?"

What's important to recognize is that most of the dechurched aren't abandoning their faith. In fact, according to research done by sociologists Josh Packard and Ashleigh Hope, those most likely to leave the church are actually the most spiritually mature and the most committed to their faith in Christ. They're not leaving the church to renounce their faith, but to preserve it. They worry that prolonged exposure to the toxicity within their church structure will sour their view of Christianity itself. Even some pastors are rethinking the systems they've built and led. "I became a pastor," one told me, "because I honestly believed the local church is the hope of the world. But now I'm not so sure." Explaining his exhaustion and fatigue, he continued, "It breaks my heart to admit this, but when I meet non-Christians in my community, I honestly think their lives will be worse, not better, if they come to my church."

Heartbreaking indeed. And yet, increasingly common. Packard and Hope refer to people like this as "church refugees."[4] They are committed Christians who feel displaced by the modern ministry machines we've built and are looking for a nurturing Christian community to call home instead. They want to know if the church must be an exhausting corporation, or if it can be a "fellowship of men and women centered on the living Christ" as it was in the beginning.

Obviously, we cannot turn back time. There is no way to re-create the church as it existed in the first century, nor should we try. We are called to *this* time, *this* culture, and *this* location. Therefore, we must ask what it means to be the church of Jesus Christ right where we are, rather than in some idealized past no longer accessible to us. I suspect answering that question will result in local churches that are very different from the ones in ancient Jerusalem, Ephesus, Corinth, or Rome.

And yet, when we turn to the words of Jesus and His apostles regarding the church, we don't see efficient, marketplace values or corporate strategies, and for an obvious reason. Those are modern ideas completely foreign to the ancient world the writers of the New Testament inhabited. Instead, the most common metaphor the biblical authors use to describe the church is a family. Unlike massive, complicated corporations, families are the most basic, but most formative, of all human communities.

And family, while a very ancient institution, remains part of our cultural framework today. Therefore, while it's wrong to read the modern idea of the church as a corporation back into Scripture, we *can* apply to our modern setting the ancient biblical idea of the church as a family.

It may sound inefficient and even quaint, but learning to view the church as a family again may prove unexpectedly relevant for the challenges of our day. Recent surveys have found that young people are experiencing an epidemic of loneliness. Despite the endless entertainment and engagement accessible to them via screens and social media, they desperately long for real, incarnate community. Increasingly, they recognize the insufficiency of technology to meet this deep need. This generation is also delaying marriage longer than any previous generation, which is contributing to their sense of disconnection.

A church that embraces the value of being a spiritual family, more than anything else, is equipped to meet this generation's relational and spiritual thirst. We are called to be an incarnate community in a world of digital avatars, a household of healing amid a culture of division and anger, and a surrogate family where a generation of spiritual orphans can find the love of Christian mothers and fathers, sisters and brothers, which ultimately points to the love of God Himself. But at precisely the moment when our society badly needs the church to rediscover the value of being a family, it has scoffed at this simple vision to chase after the dehumanizing values of corporations instead.

The goal of this book isn't to prescribe a particular church model, nor to settle matters of theological debate between divergent church traditions. Instead, I want to remind us all, re-gardless of our Christian heritage, what Jesus intended for His church to be. That means looking behind the layers of history to the essential qualities and practices of the church outlined by Jesus Himself, and then reapplying these to whatever context we find ourselves in.

Whether you are unchurched, dechurched, or someplace in between, my hope is that you will come to understand your valuable place in God's family and the valuable calling of God's family in our world. Let's begin . . .

PART 1

THE FAMILY REUNION

One of those days Jesus went out to a mountainside to pray and spent the night praying to God. When morning came, he called his disciples to him and chose twelve of them, whom he also designated apostles: Simon (whom he named Peter), his brother Andrew, James, John, Philip, Bartholomew, Matthew, Thomas, James son of Alphaeus, Simon who was called the Zealot, Judas son of James, and Judas Iscariot, who became a traitor.

He went down with them and stood on a level place. A large crowd of his disciples was there and a great number of people from all over Judea, from Jerusalem, and from the coastal region around Tyre and Sidon, who had come to hear him and to be healed of their diseases. Those troubled by impure spirits were cured, and the people all tried to touch him, because power was coming from him and healing them all.

How Do You Define "Church"

A.
BUILDING

B.
EVENT

C.
ORGANIZATION

D.
A COMMUNITY
LIVING IN UNION
W/ JESUS CHRIST
& EACH OTHER.

1 **IF JESUS WAS SERIOUS . . .
THEN WE MUST BE DEDICATED TO A
COMMUNITY AND NOT MERELY AN
INSTITUTION.**

THERE ARE FOUR DIFFERENT WAYS we use the word
church in English. First, we can mean a building where religious activities occur. (Did you see the new church being built
on Main Street?) Second, it may refer to an event. (I missed you
at church last Sunday.) Third, we use *church* when speaking of

an institution with leaders, budgets, programs, and structures. (How much did you donate to the church last year?) Finally, the word *church* is used to identify a community—the women, men, and children redeemed by Christ living in unity with Him and each other. (The church helped us through a difficult time in our marriage.)

Which is the right definition?

That's not really the best question. Depending on the context, any one of these four definitions may be appropriate. The better question to ask is: *How did the writers of the New Testament define the church?*

Anyone who has read even portions of the New Testament probably realizes Jesus and His apostles never equate the church with a building or an event. As an unrecognized and illegal religion, there were no buildings dedicated to the worship of Jesus Christ in the Roman Empire until the fourth century— well after the New Testament was written. And while the early Christians did meet weekly for prayer, teaching, and encouragement, these events were not called "church" but rather were understood to be gatherings *of* the church.

It's the other two definitions of *church* that we have a much harder time distinguishing between today. Contemporary Christians often confuse and conflate the institutional structures of a local church and the spiritual community of God's people. It is very possible to dedicate your time, treasure, and talents to an institution called a "church" but never know the mutual love, joy, hope, and support that comes when united with God's people. Likewise, organizational structures are important. We see these begin to take shape very early in the New Testament, but confusing the church with the structures designed to support it can lead to very dangerous things.

For example, the Bible is clear that the Spirit of God dwells within and among Christ's people, not within institutional structures. People are the vessels of God's presence, not programs. When we lose sight of this truth, it becomes all too easy to devote ourselves to the perpetuation of a particular ministry rather than to the people the ministry was intended to serve. Or we may come to believe God cares most about a certain structure, and then see His people as instruments for maintaining it when in fact it's precisely the opposite. God cares most about His people, and the structures of ministry exist to serve them.

As useful and important as institutions are, we must not forget that they exist only to foster the incarnate human connections through which the work of God is ultimately accomplished. In our highly systems-oriented, institutional age we need the discernment to recognize the difference between serving the church, serving the church through an institution, and merely serving an institution.

READ MORE: Acts 2:42–47; Ephesians 2:11–22

2 IF JESUS WAS SERIOUS . . . THEN WE MUST REMEMBER IT'S HIS CHURCH AND NOT OURS.

AMONG MARKETPLACE AND CHURCH LEADERS, two groups I often find myself with, there is a phrase you will hear a lot. "You've got to get the right people on your bus." It's a metaphor made popular by author and organizational guru Jim Collins. After studying why some businesses are able to achieve great success, Collins showed that it's about assembling the best team—getting the right people on your bus.

I think there is a lot of wisdom to Collins's ideas, but I also think they get over-applied to the church. Businesses recruit, hire, promote, fire, and replace in order to assemble the best team. And while many churches also apply these marketplace strategies in an effort to get the right people on the bus, they often forget one critical fact—it's not *their* bus. The bus belongs to Jesus, and He decides who is on it even if we think they're not the "right people."

To inaugurate the kingdom of God and the reconciliation of all things, Jesus assembled a team of misfits and malcontents. They were not wise or affluent. They were not powerful or influential. To make matters worse, they didn't even share the same values, background, or politics with one another. They had no earthly reason to be together.

Consider Matthew the tax collector and Simon the Zealot. Matthew was a Jew who worked for the Romans to take money from his own countrymen. He would have been seen as a traitor and selfish opportunist. Simon, on the other hand, was a freedom fighter, willing to take up arms to fight against the Roman occupiers.

For Jesus to call both Simon and Matthew into the same community, to be His disciples and to love one another, was absurd. No one thought a tax collector and a Zealot belonged on the same bus. And yet, after Jesus' resurrection, we read that His disciples "with one accord were devoting themselves to prayer" (Acts 1:14).

Unity is not something we find through a common interest, a mutual ethnic identity, a shared political ideology, or even a joint mission. It only comes from abiding in the same Lord. Left to ourselves, we would never associate with people we do not like. We would define the "right people" very differently than our Lord did, and we would probably remove the very people from the bus that He most wants on board.

This, after all, is precisely what we're seeing in the wider American culture. An increasing number of people believe the country would be better if it did not include those who hold the opposite political or cultural views. Sadly, this same viewpoint infects many churches, and Christians in those congregations need to ask themselves what bus they think they're on.

If your church is a homogeneous group who all share the same vision of society, politics, and culture, and if you chafe at the thought that you may be worshiping alongside someone who voted for a candidate you despise, or if anger arises when you discover a leader in your church prioritizes issues differently than you do—it's a pretty good indication that you haven't gotten onto Jesus' bus. Instead, you may have invited Him onto yours.

READ MORE Acts 1:12–14; 1 Corinthians 1:10–13

3 IF JESUS WAS SERIOUS . . . THEN HE HAS RECONCILED A PEOPLE, AND NOT JUST INDIVIDUALS, TO GOD.

CAN I HAVE A RELATIONSHIP WITH GOD without going to church? Church leaders want people to believe that church participation is important and that committing to a local congregation is part of one's Christian duty. On the other hand, the American church—perhaps more than any other—has emphasized having a "personal relationship with Jesus Christ," even though such language is not found in Scripture. The notion that it's just "me and God" fits our romantic notions of rugged individualism. Our culture champions the independent spirit of the explorer, the cowboy, the pioneer, and the entrepreneur. So, it makes sense that in the religious realm, American culture would also emphasize the individual's connection to God.

Some biblical characters appear to fit this pattern of "me and God." Think of Moses facing down the power of Egypt, or David defying the might of Goliath and the Philistine army. Daniel stands his ground repeatedly while exiled in Babylon, and eventually gets thrown to the lions as a result. Each of these stories fits our cultural narrative of the heroic individual whose faith compels him to defy both the odds and popular opinion. But a closer inspection of Scripture may reveal that the "me and God" framework is one we've imposed *on* the text rather than one we've learned *from* the text.

A closer look at Daniel's faith, for example, reveals an important challenge to our assumptions about having a "personal relationship" with God. Daniel is an unusual character in the Bible. He is one of the very few heroes without a blemish on his record. Nearly every Old Testament figure (Noah, Abraham, Moses, David, etc.) failed in a significant way or sinned dramatically against God. But not Daniel. I'm not saying Daniel never sinned, only that it's never recorded in Scripture. He seems to epitomize the rugged, righteous, individual faith our culture esteems.

That's why his prayer, recorded in Daniel 9, is so remarkable. Notice the pronouns he uses: "Lord, the great and awesome God . . . *we* have sinned and done wrong. *We* have

27

been wicked and have rebelled; *we* have turned away from your commands and laws. *We* have not listened to your servants the prophets . . . *we* are covered with shame . . . because of *our* unfaithfulness to you. *We* and *our* kings, *our* princes and *our* ancestors are covered with shame, LORD, because *we* have sinned against you" (Dan. 9:4–8 NIV, emphasis added).

Daniel's prayer is accurate—God's people were guilty of sin, but there is no evidence that Daniel himself ever participated in their wickedness. So, why is he including himself in their guilt? It's because Daniel recognized a facet of relating to God that we often overlook. While we have a "personal relationship with Jesus Christ," we also have a collective relationship with Him. It's not just "me and God," it's also "us and God." Belonging to Christ also means belonging to His people. Sharing in His glory also means sharing in their guilt. Calling God our Father also means calling those within the church our sisters and brothers. The testimony of the Bible is clear that Jesus is not merely reconciling separate individuals but *a people* to God.

 READ MORE **Daniel 9:4–8; 1 Corinthians 12:14–16**

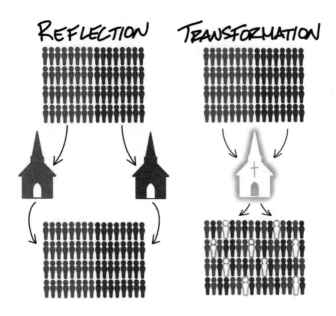

REFLECTION   TRANSFORMATION

4 IF JESUS WAS SERIOUS . . . THEN HIS CHURCH SHOULD MEND SOCIAL DIVISIONS, NOT REFLECT THEM.

THE CHURCH IS CALLED to courageously and prophetically overcome the divisions of the world, but all too often it merely reflects and reinforces them. In the mid-twentieth century, as the United States was slowly integrating after centuries of racial segregation, Martin Luther King Jr. observed that eleven o'clock Sunday morning remained "the most segregated hour in this nation." What might surprise you is that King's statement, which was made over fifty years ago, is just as true today.

Lifeway Research has found that 86 percent of congregations in the US remain racially homogeneous. That's a slight improvement from the 97 percent in an earlier study. While that trajectory is encouraging, the more troubling finding from the survey was that most Christians still *prefer* a racially segregated church. The report said, "Surprisingly, most churchgoers are content with the ethnic status quo in their churches. In a world where our culture is increasingly diverse, and many pastors are talking about diversity, it appears most people are happy where they are—and with whom they are."[5]

There are many explanations for the racial homogeneity seen in most churches, and many books have been written about it. Of course, the most obvious and innocent explanation is that some churches are located in racially homogeneous communities. It's unlikely your church will be more diverse than the town in which it is located. But even in more diverse communities, most congregations remain homogeneous, and this is not fueled by overt or even subconscious racism. Instead, it's driven by pragmatism. It's far easier to lead, manage, and operate a single-culture church where there is broad agreement about music styles, program structures, leadership, and values, and historically churches have grown faster and larger when they are homogeneous. Birds of a feather, the data says, like to fellowship together.

But when we look at Jesus' first followers and the earliest Christians through whom God shook the world, we do not see a church that valued pragmatism over diversity. For example, even within the very small sample of the twelve Jesus called to be closest to Him, we discover a shocking amount of diversity. As has been said, Simon was a Zealot—a Jewish freedom fighter willing to use violence to overthrow Roman occupation—and Matthew was a tax collector—a Jew who betrayed his own people to make money by working for the Romans.

And yet, Jesus called both of these men not only to be His disciples, but He called them to embrace each other as brothers. What united Simon and Matthew wasn't a common political, cultural, or economic vision. It was Jesus and nothing else. God calling these two men together wasn't practical, but it was beautiful. Isn't that what the church, and the world, need right now?

 READ MORE: Ephesians 4:1–6; Luke 6:12–19

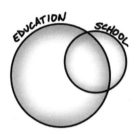

"I NEVER LET SCHOOLING INTERFERE WITH MY EDUCATION."
— MARK TWAIN

"NEVER LET CHURCH STRUCTURES LIMIT YOUR COMMUNION WITH GOD."
— SKYE JETHANI

5 IF JESUS WAS SERIOUS . . . THEN OUR GOAL SHOULD BE MORE THAN ATTENDING CHURCH.

LIKE MANY OTHER FAMILIES, our normal routines were significantly impacted by the pandemic in 2020. My kids were in middle school, high school, and college at the time. For much of the year, none of their schools were meeting in person. Thankfully, with or without entering a school building or sitting in a classroom, everyone agreed that their education had to continue. The unusual circumstances surrounding the COVID-19 pandemic reminded many of us that education and schooling are not synonymous. As Mark Twain reportedly said, "I never let my schooling interfere with my education." During 2020, my parental responsibility was to educate my kids, not just school them.

Just as the pandemic taught us of the difference between school (an institution) and education (the institution's purpose), we need to have a similar awakening about the church. As mentioned earlier, about thirty years ago, a new word entered our Christian lexicon that has blurred the line between the church institution and its purpose. Prior generations spoke about believers or unbelievers, Christians and non-Christians, but today it's not uncommon to speak of the *churched* or *unchurched*. I worry that this language, which is incredibly common among pastors, conflates the institution with its purpose. It assumes the goal is to get someone "churched" and that success is the perpetuation of the institution itself. This is a shortsighted vision, like a school awarding diplomas merely for attending rather than for learning.

Just as it is possible to attend school and not be educated, it is entirely possible to be churched and not be living in communion with Christ—especially when *church* is defined institutionally rather than communally. The church has a vital and undeniable role to play in our spiritual formation—one that too many Christians ignore. At the same time, the institutional church cannot be the only source for our development as Christians and it cannot encompass the entirety of our life with God. There are other resources, relationships, personal practices, and acts of service that draw us into deeper communion with Christ beyond Sunday morning worship or the programs of our local congregation. Just as our education is bigger than our school, so our life with God must be bigger than the institution of the church.

Back in 2014, we took our kids out of school to travel overseas. For those few weeks, we concluded their education would be advanced more by *not* attending school—and their teachers agreed. They recognized the ultimate goal was education, not just school attendance, and the teachers worked with us to develop a customized plan for all three kids. It was a wonderful example of thoughtful and caring people putting the goal and the institution in their proper places.

Likewise, the institutional church is an incredible gift, but we must remember that it is a means to an end. The institution does not exist for itself.

 READ MORE: 2 Peter 1:3–9; John 4:19–26

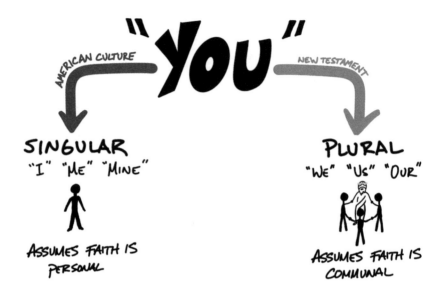

6 IF JESUS WAS SERIOUS . . . THEN FOLLOWING JESUS ISN'T ABOUT ME, IT'S ABOUT US.

IN CASE YOU WERE UNAWARE, the Bible was not written in the twenty-first century, nor was it written in English. It is an ancient book (technically it's a collection of ancient books) originally composed in Hebrew (Old Testament) and Greek (New Testament). While most modern English versions are incredibly well researched and composed, inevitably some things get lost in translation.

For example, there is no unique second-person plural

pronoun in English. We say "you" whether speaking to an individual or to a group (except in the South where "y'all" attempts to fill in the gap). This lack of nuance in English, when combined with our strong cultural value of individualism, can profoundly warp the way we read Scripture.

Most of the apostolic letters, which make up most of the New Testament, were not written to individuals but to churches. Therefore, when we encounter the word "you" in these writings it is most often *plural*, but the English reader has no way of knowing that apart from the wider context and an awareness of the apostle's original audience. Simply put, in most cases, the apostles are not speaking to *me*, but to *us*. They were instructing communities and only rarely commanding individuals. A significant amount of the Bible's teaching makes little sense or can be dangerously misapplied if divorced from a communal vision of Christian faith.

Unfortunately, that is exactly what many of us do. Our American individualism combined with the limitations of English mean we often assume the text is speaking to *me*, and the corporate application the apostles intended is far from our imaginations. Our minds are simply not trained to think collectively, so we tend to confine and individualize the text. We emphasize the "personal relationship with God" bias of consumeristic Christianity and overlook our corporate identity as a member of Christ's body—the church.

Most of us are never going to learn Greek or Hebrew, and we can't just change the English language. (Although teenagers are trying—when did "literally" start to mean "figuratively"?) That means we need to engage Scripture carefully with an awareness of our own cultural biases and blind spots. We need to slow down every time we encounter the word "you" in a New Testament letter and ask ourselves not only how this applies to *me*, but also what it means for *us*.

 READ MORE: **1 Corinthians 3:5–19; 1 Peter 2:4–10**

BELIEVERS

SKEPTICS

"BELIEVERS ARGUE WITH GOD; SKEPTICS ARGUE WITH EACH OTH[ER]
—EUGENE PETERSO[N]

7 IF JESUS WAS SERIOUS . . . THEN CHURCH IS WHERE WE WRESTLE WITH GOD TOGETHER.

MARTIN LUTHER KING JR. SAID, "The arc of the moral universe is long, but it bends toward justice."[6] In my darker moments, however, I can doubt this claim. Because the arc is long, I often fail to recognize its curve and my imagination can feed the fear that there is no arc at all. What if there is no bend toward justice? What if I am a fool following the imaginary calling of a nonexistent God? What frightens me most isn't facing

42

hardship or pain, but the possibility that my pain has no purpose. What if everything really is meaningless?

This is the central struggle of faith. Is there a God-directed arc to the universe; a purpose that is hidden but will be revealed with time? Or is the arc itself an illusion and the cosmos ruled by an unsympathetic, unbending line perpetually pointing at chaos?

As we face the trials and triumphs of life, we all wrestle with that question in our souls—both believers and nonbelievers, Christians and atheists. Some think that to believe in God means no longer struggling with these deep questions of meaning, that somehow the true Christian never knows doubt. That is untrue. Being a Christian simply means we've shifted the focus of our struggle. As Eugene Peterson said, "Believers argue with God; skeptics argue with each other."[7]

In the Old Testament, Jacob was a very flawed man full of doubts and fears. These insecurities led him to seek control by manipulating others. He was a notorious cheat and liar. One night, in a vision, Jacob encountered God in the form of a man. Jacob wrestled with the Lord all night, trying to force God to bless him and alleviate his fears. Eventually, Jacob surrendered in his attempt to take God's blessing and trusted Him instead. Before he woke, the Lord gave him a new name—Israel, which means *wrestles with God*.

Jacob's story epitomizes the life of faith. God's people trust Him, but it's often a struggle because we are flawed, fearful creatures. A church—being an assembly of believers—is simply a community that wrestles with God together. It's where we struggle openly rather than privately, and where questions are asked and sometimes answered. But when no answer is found, the church is also where we find comfort, support, and encouragement. It's where we are reminded in our worship and in our fellowship that the arc is long, and although we don't always see it, there is a curve and it does bend toward justice.

READ MORE: Genesis 32:22–28; Romans 12:3–8

PRAYER ⟶ COMMUNITY

8 IF JESUS WAS SERIOUS . . . THEN CHURCH IS WHERE WE FIND— AND PRAY FOR—OUR ENEMIES.

WHAT MAKES A COMMUNITY "CHRISTIAN"? Justin Martyr, a second-century church father, described the Christian community this way: "We who formerly hated and murdered one another . . . now live together and share the same table. Now we pray for our enemies and try to win those who hate us."[8] Justin Martyr recognized the power of the gospel to reconcile people to one another as well as to God. For him, and many other early Christians, faith in Jesus Christ was not an individual, privatized devotion. It manifested itself boldly in the social and public square. It fundamentally changed the way people saw, and embraced, one another.

That power is needed today more than ever. There is no question we are a deeply divided society, and the divisions are more than political. With the proliferation of social media and algorithms that severely narrow our vision of the world, we seem to occupy completely different realities. The result isn't just an inability to understand others' beliefs, but the erosion of empathy for those we disagree with. This is why we increasingly see a neighbor as a nemesis and a political opponent as the embodiment of evil. With the aid of technology, divisions today don't merely separate us, they dehumanize us.

Rather than reflecting the divisions of society, the church is called to reflect the unity of God's kingdom. Echoing the command of Jesus, Justin Martyr said those engaged in a true Christian community will pray for their enemies. This transformative act not only benefits the enemy being prayed for but also the Christian who is praying because it is not possible to pray on behalf of someone and simultaneously hate him. We cannot implore our Lord to both bless and curse our opponent. In prayer, goodwill grows to eclipse malice in the heart of the Christian toward her enemy.

I wonder how different our churches would be if we actively prayed for those we perceive to be opposed to us? And that doesn't mean praying for their failure or destruction, but earnestly praying for their blessing and well-being. How might we detoxify our souls from the fear and anger we've absorbed from cable news or social media if our worship gatherings included

WHAT IF JESUS WAS SERIOUS ABOUT THE CHURCH?

just a few minutes of sincere prayer like that? How might this essential discipline of the church begin a movement of healing and reconciliation in our diverse and divided communities?

Justin Martyr understood that praying for our enemies is the first step in changing how we see them. And once we see them differently, they might just come to see us differently as well. This process, when fueled by God's Spirit, ultimately leads to former enemies living in the same community of faith and sharing the same table of fellowship. That means the church's greatest weapon against evil isn't how we *vote* but how we *pray*.

 READ MORE: **1 Peter 3:8–12; James 3:13–18**

9 IF JESUS WAS SERIOUS . . . THEN THE CHURCH IS UNITED IN LOVE, NOT ANGER.

RECENTLY, I WATCHED A DOCUMENTARY about the relationship between William F. Buckley, the father of the modern conservative movement, and Gore Vidal, a liberal intellectual novelist. The film was appropriately titled *Best of Enemies*. The two men hated each other with a stunning purity. In 1968, they did a series of television appearances together to debate the presidential election and the philosophical direction of the country.

In the footage, their contempt for one another is palpable and sometimes audible.

The film reminded me how powerful hatred can be, particularly when focused on a single person or group. Anger is so visceral, and far more accessible for most of us than empathy or reason, that it's the emotion we usually experience first when challenged. When we feel out of control, fearful, or even mildly uncomfortable, anger appears almost instantaneously. And this anger isn't generalized—it's focused on whatever or whomever we perceive to be the cause of our struggle.

For this reason, anger has been elevated to a virtue in much of our culture. With it, we are able to define ourselves by who we stand against, rather than the ideals we stand for. In a twisted way, we have become dependent on our enemies. They give our lives definition, our beliefs boundaries, and our mission an opponent. For many people today, including those who identify as Christians, enemies are what give our lives and communities meaning.

Of course, this is not a new phenomenon. There's an old saying of uncertain origin that says, "A friend is someone who has the same enemies you have." It has always been our sinful human nature to organize our social lives around those who share our fears and prejudices. This was no less evident in the ancient world of the Bible where Jews defined themselves by who they were not. They were not filthy, idol-worshiping, sexually immoral, pork-eating, unrighteous, and scripturally ignorant Gentiles. Their contempt for non-Jews was so strong that Gentiles were often referred to as "dogs." And, of course, the hatred was mutual. Many Gentiles harbored contempt and disdain for Jews who did not join in the practices and worship of the Roman Empire.

Imagine the shock, therefore, when a new community emerged where Jews and Gentiles worshiped together, shared a table, and called one another "brothers and sisters." It was scandalous and even shameful. Rather than defining themselves by their hatred for the other group, within the church both Jews and Gentiles learned to release their hate and instead define themselves based on Christ's love.

We ought to be very suspicious of any leaders who use anger to motivate us, or who demonize certain individuals or groups as a way of defining those who are "true believers." These tactics, while certainly effective in a worldly sense, do not conform to the example of Christ or His first followers. The early church was not driven by anger, nor were Jesus' followers defined by their enemies. Instead, they were compelled by God's love and defined by the cross where Jesus willingly gave up His life to save His enemies.

 READ MORE: Ephesians 2:11–22; 2 Corinthians 5:14–19

PART 2:

THE FAMILY MEAL

When the hour came, Jesus and his apostles reclined at the table. And he said to them, "I have eagerly desired to eat this Passover with you before I suffer. For I tell you, I will not eat it again until it finds fulfillment in the kingdom of God."

After taking the cup, he gave thanks and said, "Take this and divide it among you. For I tell you I will not drink again from the fruit of the vine until the kingdom of God comes."

And he took bread, gave thanks and broke it, and gave it to them, saying, "This is my body given for you; do this in remembrance of me."

In the same way, after the supper he took the cup, saying, "This cup is the new covenant in my blood, which is poured out for you."

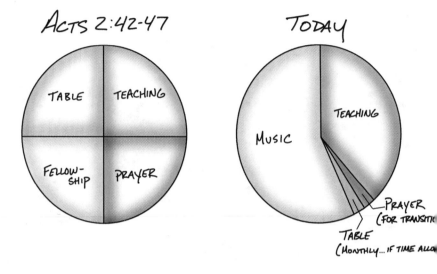

ACTS 2:42-47

TABLE | TEACHING
FELLOW-SHIP | PRAYER

TODAY

MUSIC

TEACHING

PRAYER (FOR TRANSITIO

TABLE (MONTHLY... IF TIME ALLO

10 IF JESUS WAS SERIOUS . . . THEN THE CHURCH CANNOT IGNORE HIS TABLE.

THE CHURCH HAS EXISTED for over two thousand years, and throughout the millennia Christians have gathered on Sundays to worship God. Across all those generations, however, very few things have remained the same. For example, the church has not always had a dedicated building to gather in. The earliest Christians met in homes. We have not always had projectors and instruments to accompany our singing. We haven't always had a complete record of the Scriptures. In the first century after Christ,

His followers received occasional letters from the apostles for instruction; there wasn't yet a complete New Testament.

And yet, across every generation, every ethnicity, every economic and denominational barrier, the simple elements of the bread and the cup have endured as marks of Christ's people. The table has united the church throughout the ages. Its origin is found in the Passover meal Jesus shared with His followers on the night of His betrayal and arrest. He used the bread and wine to communicate the meaning of His impending death. He was offering Himself as a sacrifice for the world's sins, and through His death opening the way for us to be united with God and one another. For that reason, the meal has always been central to the Christian life and any exploration of the church must consider Christ's table, its meaning, its place in our worship, and how it forms our life with God and one another.

Of course, a shared meal is not uniquely Christian. The table is a powerful tool in every culture because every society uses meals to both unite and divide. Sharing a table is how we form bonds and establish a common identity. It's why every culture uses a meal to celebrate marriages. Two families share a meal to acknowledge their new bond as kin. Likewise, every culture uses the table to divide and exclude. Segregation in the American South prohibited blacks from eating in public with whites to solidify their status as unequal and enforce a belief in racial hierarchy.

The unifying and dividing power of food is also a dominant theme in the Bible. In the beginning, the Lord invited the man and woman to eat from any tree in the garden, but eating from one particular tree would separate them from God and life itself. And the Old Testament dietary laws, which seem odd and arbitrary to modern readers, had a very practical function. They prevented the Israelites from sharing a menu, and therefore a table, with the nations surrounding them. If people are unable to eat together, they are less likely to form bonds, blend cultures, or intermarry. Israel's odd diet kept them separate, thereby preserving their special calling and covenant with God.

Sharing a meal is a bodily, social, creative, and spiritual act perhaps second only to sex in its power to form bonds. A church that ignores this power, or uses it in a manner contrary to the gospel, does so to its own peril. But for Christians who recognize the formative power of the table, it can be used by God to shape their lives and community in unimaginably beautiful ways.

 READ MORE: **Leviticus 11:1–10; Acts 2:42–47**

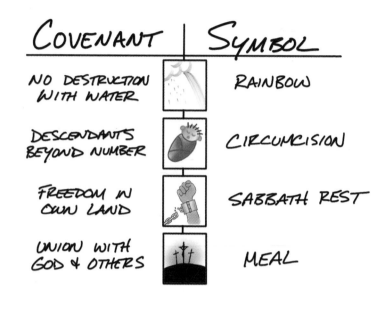

Covenant	Symbol
No destruction with water	Rainbow
Descendants beyond number	Circumcision
Freedom in own land	Sabbath rest
Union with God & others	Meal

11 IF JESUS WAS SERIOUS . . . THEN A SYMBOL IS NEVER JUST A SYMBOL.

I DO NOT UNDERSTAND those who dismiss the Lord's Table as "just a symbol." A symbol by definition represents something more than what it is. For example, if an American flag were not a symbol, it would merely be a red, white, and blue cloth, but because it *is* a symbol it carries powerful and emotional meaning for millions of people. Being a symbol always makes something *more* important and never less. The same is true for Christ's table.

During the Passover meal with His disciples, Jesus said the cup of wine represented "the new covenant in my blood." He was elevating the meal as a new covenant symbol—a concept that would have been familiar to His Jewish followers. Throughout the Old Testament, God's relationship with His people developed through a series of covenants—agreements and promises—and each one was marked with a symbol related to the nature of the covenant itself.

After the flood, for example, the Lord promised to never destroy the world again with water, and He used a rainbow as a sign of this covenant. Later, He promised Abraham, who was old and had no children, that he would have descendants beyond number. This covenant was symbolized by circumcision—a mark on the part of the body necessary for reproduction. And when God rescued His people from slavery and gave them His law, He instructed them to rest one day every week. The Sabbath, according to Deuteronomy 5:15, was a symbol so the people would remember how the Lord had rescued them from the brutality of slavery. Egyptian slaves, after all, never got a day off from work.

In each case, the covenant symbol was directly related to the nature of the covenant itself, and each symbol pointed to something powerful about God's relationship with His people. Rainbows/flood, circumcision/children, rest/slavery. Therefore, the fact that Jesus identified a communal meal as the "sign" of God's new covenant with His people actually magnifies its importance. The fact that the table is a symbol is precisely why it should be central to the life of the church, and never used as a reason to ignore or dismiss it as some Christian communities are inclined to do.

A shared meal is a powerful reminder that what Jesus accomplished on the cross wasn't a sacrifice merely to redeem *me*, but the way God has reconciled *a people* to Himself. As we look at our sisters and brothers around the Lord's Table, we are reminded that the new covenant is how Christ has brought reconciliation between hostile people, not just between individuals and God.

 READ MORE: Deuteronomy 5:12–15; Ephesians 2:11–16

THE WORLD

THE CHURCH

"CLIMB!"

"COME!"

**IF JESUS WAS SERIOUS . . .
THEN WE EXPERIENCE THE REALITY
OF HIS KINGDOM THROUGH THE
TABLE.**

MY BEST FRIEND IN HIGH SCHOOL, Jay, had a theory to explain the social stratification of our school. He believed the most important moment of our adolescent social lives happened when we entered the lunchroom on the first day of junior high school. Kids from four different elementary schools were mixed together for the first time, and most of us randomly picked a table. The table you chose, Jay argued, defined your friends, and your social status, for the next seven years. Some chose a lunch table in the center of the cafeteria, which, it turned out, was destined for popularity and acclaim. I was drawn to a table in the corner with the other introverts that was doomed for obscurity.

Much like my junior high lunchroom, ancient Israel used the table to define a person's community and identity. Who you ate with determined your social status and your destiny, and being welcomed to a table was also a powerful sign of unity and reconciliation. The ancient world, in a way, was a giant lunchroom, and each table was ranked. The righteous religious leaders were at the top of this hierarchy, and the most egregious sinners were the losers in the corner. This table-based ranking of society is critical to understanding Jesus' ministry.

Before He was identified as the Messiah, Jesus was widely heralded as a brilliant rabbi. Other religious leaders, however, were disturbed by Jesus' eagerness to share His table with outcasts—tax collectors, prostitutes, sinners, and other ne'er-do-wells pushed to the margins of respectable society. This was not the behavior of a reputable teacher, let alone one who was seen as a prophet of God. In fact, Jesus' dinner guests became a source of repeated controversy and debate. Some even pointed to His lunch table choice as proof that He was not a prophet, because by eating with known sinners He was elevating their status and diminishing His own.

We often look at Jesus' habit of sharing a table with sinners as a reflection of His grace and hospitality. It was certainly that, but there's another dimension we must not overlook. Theologian Wolfhart Pannenberg says it this way: "We have in these meals the central symbolic action of Jesus in which his message of the nearness of God's reign and its salvation is focused and vividly depicted. . . . Everything that separates from God is removed in the table fellowship that Jesus practiced."[9] In other words, the essence of Jesus' message was manifested in His meals.

Jesus preached that God's kingdom was at hand; it was near and He called everyone to enter into it. He often used parables about banquets and meals to illustrate the kingdom's inclusivity and abundance. But for Jesus, this was more than a message, and the table was more than a sermon illustration. It was the pattern and practice of His life. His eagerness to welcome everyone to His table, even those farthest from God, was how the presence of the kingdom was revealed and how the established hierarchy of the world's lunchroom was being turned upside down, and He has called the church to use His table no differently.

 READ MORE: Matthew 9:10–13; Luke 14:7–11

LORD'S TABLE

CHRIST IS KING

COFFEE BAR

CUSTOMER IS KING

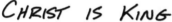

13 IF JESUS WAS SERIOUS . . . THEN WE MUST NOT REPLACE HIS TABLE WITH A COFFEE BAR.

ALTHOUGH THE TABLE WAS CENTRAL to Jesus' mission, and the table has been the only consistent element throughout two thousand years of Christian worship, in many contemporary churches it has largely disappeared. Today, some churches have marginalized the Lord's Table to a monthly practice tagged on to the end of a gathering. In others, especially more market-oriented and larger ministries, the table has disappeared altogether. Customer focus groups showed its symbolism was a barrier to newcomers, and the logistics of serving ten thousand or more attendees each weekend proved too cumbersome. Ironically, for attendees of some churches, the central component of Jesus' ministry is now seen as an impediment to theirs.

Earlier we looked at how meals are a universal human activity and the primary way every culture creates bonds and constructs identity. When Christians no longer form these bonds around the bread and cup, which represent Jesus' sacrifice, we shouldn't be surprised when something else takes its place. According to Paul Louis Metzger, a professor of theology and culture, the coffee bar has replaced the Communion table in many churches, with unintended consequences.

Located in many church foyers and ranging from a small drink station with donut holes to a full café rivaling Starbucks, the church coffee bar is where we gather, connect, and participate in ritual consumption. Not only does the coffee bar serve the practical function of caffeinating the congregation—a requirement for those with loquacious preachers—it also creates a welcoming atmosphere for conversation and connection. For these reasons, a church coffee bar can be a blessing.

But the coffee bar also carries a danger, especially for those congregations that have abandoned the regular practice of the Lord's Table. As Metzger recognizes, "Both the coffee bar and Lord's Table affirm community, but the *kind* of community they affirm differs significantly"[10] (emphasis added). At the Lord's Table, we are guests; we are each invited and welcomed by Christ. We do not choose who we share the meal with. We do not place an order. We do not customize our beverage. Instead, we all receive the same bread and drink from the same cup. At the Lord's Table, we are all humble recipients of the same un-merited grace.

At the coffee bar, by contrast, we are in control. We review our options. We order what we want, when we want, and how we want. We decide whom to share a table with, and whom to avoid. The coffee bar is not designed to form us into Christians, but into *consumers*. This doesn't mean coffee bars in churches are wrong. As I've already noted, they have many benefits. But they cannot be a substitute for the Table of Christ, and when a church coffee bar is a permanent fixture and the Lord's Table is an infrequent practice, we shouldn't be surprised which one shapes our lives more. As Metzger notes, "Churches with coffee bars may have to work harder to ensure they are foster-ing community around the values of Christ rather than casual consumerism."[11]

 READ MORE: 1 Corinthians 11:17–22; Isaiah 55:1–3

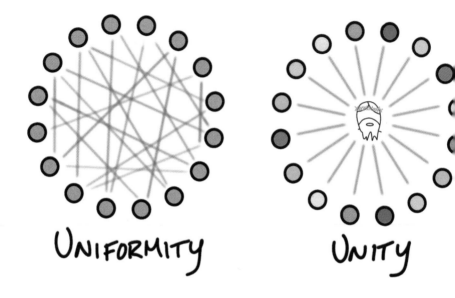

UNIFORMITY   UNITY

14 IF JESUS WAS SERIOUS . . . THEN THE PERSON YOU LIKE LEAST WILL BE AT HIS TABLE.

ABOUT THIRTY YEARS AGO, a team of researchers began studying church growth. They observed that the fastest growing churches often lacked diversity. Instead, these churches were filled with people who shared the same race, economic status, culture, and values. The explanation for this is simple—we are most comfortable in groups filled with people just like us. Therefore, a group is likely to grow faster if everyone within it is the same. The researchers called it the "Homogeneous Unit Principle."

What they intended as an observation, however, was made into a prescription for church growth by ambitious pastors. Ministry professionals took the data and said if you want your church to grow, *avoid diversity*. Of course, it was rarely presented that negatively. Instead, churches were advised to "define your target audience" or plant congregations in homogeneous suburbs rather than in more diverse urban areas. Pastors were coached to design their churches to appeal to a single demographic. That way, when newcomers enter the church, they'd discover it's already filled with people who live, think, spend, vote, and look just like them. There is no doubt the Homogeneous Unit Principle *works*, but a more important question rarely gets asked—is it *right*? Does it fit with the church we find in the New Testament?

The biggest controversy facing the first followers of Jesus was how to integrate Jewish and Gentile Christians into one community. Everyone would have preferred homogeneous congregations with Jews and Gentiles occupying separate churches where each could preserve their cultures, languages, and traditions without disruption or compromise. Everyone would have preferred a church where Jews shared a table with other Jews, and where Gentiles shared a table with other Gentiles. After all, this was the established practice in the Roman Empire and the law among Jews. No doubt homogeneous churches would have been easier to lead, more conducive for growth, and less controversial.

But that's not the church Jesus wanted. Instead, He called

Jews and Gentiles to share one faith, one church, and one table. As a committed Jew, the apostle Peter struggled repeatedly with seeing Gentiles as his equals. It took visions and manifestations of the Spirit's power to convince him people unlike him were also welcomed by God, and his habit of only eating with Jews required a rebuke from another apostle before Peter changed his behavior.

Like us, Peter wanted a comfortable church filled with the people he preferred. He wanted the Communion table to be occupied by people who shared his identity and his views. But the church doesn't belong to us; it belongs to Christ. And the table is not ours; it is the Lord's. And the community He is building looks nothing like the one we would choose. As Parker Palmer wrote:

> In true community we will not choose our companions, for our choices are so often limited by self-serving motives. Instead, our companions will be given to us by grace. Often they will be persons who will upset our settled view of self and world. In fact, we might define true community as that place where the person you least want to live with lives.[12]

 READ MORE: **Acts 10:9–28; Galatians 3:25–29**

TIME MACHINES

POWER REQUIRED: 1.21 GIGAWATTS

POWER REQUIRED: COMMUNITY OF FAITH

15 IF JESUS WAS SERIOUS . . . THEN HIS TABLE IS A TIME MACHINE.

JESUS COMMANDED HIS FOLLOWERS to break bread and share the cup "in remembrance" of Him. Using commonly available items like bread and wine to remember Jesus made sense in the ancient world, but today we have far better tools available. We have video screens, streaming sermons, and mass publishing. We have Christian T-shirts, bracelets, and avatars. We have little Jesus-fish on our cars eating little Darwin-fish with legs. We have so many things to remind us of Jesus; do we really need the Communion table anymore?

Well, that depends on what Jesus meant by "remembrance." If remembering is merely an act of mental recollection, which is how modern people understand it, then the Lord's Table seems unnecessary and redundant. The ancient Jewish understanding of *remembrance*, however, was very different from ours. Theologian Paul Bradshaw puts it this way: "In the Jewish world, remembrance was not a purely mental activity . . . it was not simply about nostalgia for the past . . . but about asking God to remember his people and *complete his saving purpose today*"[13] (emphasis added).

In the ancient world, remembrance was not merely the mental recollection of past events. Rather, it meant recalling a past event *so that the power of that event may enter the present.* For Jesus and His disciples, the redemptive work of God was not something to reminisce about. It was not just a story to be mentally recalled. The redemption of God, and His power to deliver His people, was continuing right into the present.

This is why Jesus celebrated the Passover meal with His friends. The Passover was a symbol of how God saved His people from slavery in the past, but Jesus appealed to that power and applied it to their present circumstances. He used the unleavened bread from the Passover meal and gave it a contemporary meaning. "This is my body, broken for you." And the same with the wine. "This is the new covenant in my blood." The meal was not just about remembering what God had done in the past—Jesus was inviting that saving power into the present.

So when Jesus told His Jewish followers to take the bread and the cup "in remembrance of me," He was instructing them to do something more than a mental exercise. The table was to be more than an edible history lesson. When we come to the table, we are not just recalling the story of Jesus' crucifixion from two thousand years ago. The table is a time machine through which God's saving power from the past is transported into the present.

If we believe the table is just a mental exercise, then it's no surprise why it's been replaced in our gathering with hypnotic videos and loud music. But what if we're wrong? What if the table isn't just about remembering God's past redemption? What if it's about *experiencing* His redemption today? What if, in remembering, we bring the salvation from the past into the present? If that's what Christ intended it to be, then by marginalizing the table in the church we have unknowingly marginalized the power of God and replaced it with a performance by mere humans.

 READ MORE: **Exodus 13:3–10; Luke 22:14–20**

PAST   FUTURE

16 IF JESUS WAS SERIOUS . . . THEN THE TABLE IS WHERE WE GLIMPSE THE FUTURE.

WE'VE SEEN HOW THE TABLE does more than commemorate the past. Based on the Hebrew understanding of remembrance, when we come to the table, we are inviting the power of God's salvation from the past to find completion in the present. But the table is more than a time machine to the past; it is also a glimpse into the future.

At the Passover meal, Jesus used the bread and wine to represent His redemptive death. The sorrow of betrayal, abandonment, and death was certainly on Jesus' mind. His hour of suffering had finally come. But there was more on His mind than the cross. He said to His friends: "I have eagerly desired to eat this Passover with you before I suffer. For I tell you I will not eat it again until it finds fulfillment in the kingdom of God." And when He had taken a cup and given thanks, He said, "Take this and divide it among you. For I tell you, I will not drink again of the fruit of the vine until the kingdom of God comes" (Luke 22:15–18 NIV).

These words reveal that Jesus was not just focused on God's past faithfulness or even His present work of redemption through the cross. He was also looking to the *future*—the fulfillment of the kingdom of God. At that Passover table with His friends, Jesus anticipated a future table, a future feast, and a future cup. On the other side of His suffering he saw a celebration. Revelation 19 offers us a glimpse of the banquet Jesus imagined. Known as the wedding feast of the Lamb, the meal represents the fulfillment of God's redemptive work in history when all evil is vanquished, the innocent are vindicated, and the world is made right.

Like Jesus, the earliest Christians saw the Communion table as a prophetic symbol; a window into a future age. For those experiencing great persecution, pain, and trials, the table offered hope. It was a foretaste of the feast that was to come in a world without pain, where we will sit at a table with no traitors, with bodies that shed neither blood nor tears, and where God Himself will serve us as His people.

Therefore, when the church comes to the table on Sunday, we do so not just to remember the past, but to remember the future. We gather to feast on the imagination of Christ—to see what He saw, to fill our minds with the sights, and sounds, and smells of heaven even if the darkness around us feels like hell. When we come to the table as Jesus did, we will discover it is where the past, present, and future converge into a single point of grace.

 READ MORE: Luke 22:14–20; Revelation 19:1–9

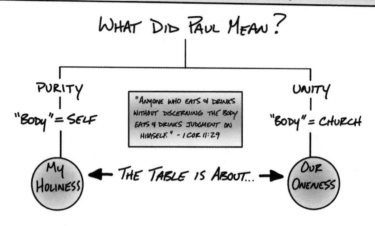

"EVERYONE OUGHT TO EXAMINE THEMSELVES BEFORE THEY EAT OF THE BREAD & DRINK FROM THE CUP" 1 COR 11:28

WHAT DID PAUL MEAN?

PURITY

"BODY" = SELF

"ANYONE WHO EATS & DRINKS WITHOUT DISCERNING THE BODY EATS & DRINKS JUDGMENT ON HIMSELF." - 1 COR 11:29

UNITY

"BODY" = CHURCH

My HOLINESS ← THE TABLE IS ABOUT... → OUR ONENESS

17 IF JESUS WAS SERIOUS . . . THEN HIS TABLE IS ABOUT CHURCH UNITY, NOT PERSONAL PURITY.

SOME WHO WERE RAISED in Christian communities were taught to fear the Lord's Table. "Examine yourself!" the minister would warn quoting the apostle Paul. "Whoever eats the bread or drinks the cup of the Lord in an unworthy manner will be guilty of profaning the body and blood of the Lord" (1 Cor. 11:27). Taken out of context, these words make the Communion table sound dangerous, like a downed power line. At least that's how I saw it as a kid. The table looked ordinary enough, but it could unleash the wrath of God upon the unworthy. As teenagers we were finally permitted to take the potentially lethal thimble of grape juice and the cracker, but only after another stern warning from Scripture: "Anyone who eats and drinks without discerning the body eats and drinks judgment on himself" (1 Cor. 11:29).

In too many churches, these verses cast a pall over Communion Sunday and turned the Lord's Table into a morbid ritual marked by the fear of judgment. Rather than the open-armed Jesus of the Gospels who welcomed sinners to His dinner table, too many of us imagine Jesus to be an intimidating maître d' ensuring only the right people get a seat and the unworthy are judged for even trying. Making matters worse, to a teenager's ear the instruction to "discern the body" before taking Communion sounded like yet another warning from the church about the inexcusable nature of sexual sin.

It wasn't until years later that I learned my assumptions about the table, and the way Paul's words from 1 Corinthians 11 were employed, were completely wrong.

Paul's primary concern with the Lord's Table was *unity*, not purity. Rather than gathering at the table as a sign of their oneness in Christ, the Corinthians were using the table to reinforce social divisions—particularly the divide in their culture between rich and poor. In the first century, the wealthy did not share a table with the poor. Jews did not eat with Greeks. Slaves did not break bread with the free. The Corinthians had uncritically carried these attitudes into the church and into their practice of the Lord's Supper. This is why Paul was so upset. Through their disunity, they were betraying the meaning of the meal. They were mocking the sacrifice of Christ, which had made them one family.

Once we understand this context, Paul's warnings take on a very different meaning and tone. The call to discern "the body" isn't about sexual purity or self-control. Throughout his letter, Paul uses the body as a metaphor for the church. That means before we come to the Lord's Table as a church, we are to discern whether there are divisions within our community. Is anyone being mistreated or marginalized? Are we coming as one people united in Christ or as those still divided by the categories of our society? And while self-examination is always beneficial, here Paul is asking us to examine whether we are estranged from a sister or brother, and to heal that division before coming to the table. Paul was simply echoing Jesus' own command from the Sermon on the Mount to leave your gift at the altar and first be reconciled to your brother before worshiping God (Matt. 5:23–24).

Ironically, our tendency to hyper-individualize our practice of the Lord's Table with warnings about sexual purity and the confession of personal sin rather than social division has contributed to the very disunity Paul warned about. To use his words, communities that make the table about *me* rather than about *us* are guilty of profaning the body and blood of the Lord.

READ MORE: 1 Corinthians 11:17–34; Matthew 5:23–24

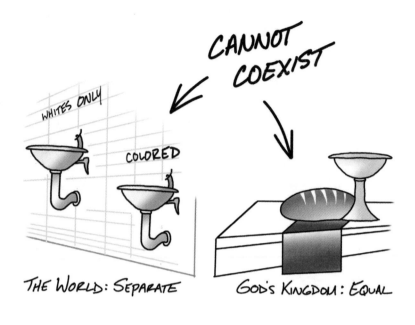

CANNOT COEXIST

WHITES ONLY

COLORED

THE WORLD: SEPARATE

GOD'S KINGDOM: EQUAL

18 IF JESUS WAS SERIOUS . . . THEN HIS TABLE WILL CONFRONT EVIL AND ESTABLISH JUSTICE.

IN 1865, NOT LONG AFTER the American Civil War ended, the members of St. Paul's Episcopal Church in Richmond, Virginia, gathered for worship. Among them were many leaders of the defeated Confederacy. When the time came for Communion, a tall, well-dressed black man walked forward to the table. "This was a great surprise and shock," a witness reported in the *Richmond Times-Dispatch*. "Its effect upon the communicants was startling, and for several moments they retained their seats in solemn silence and did not move, being deeply chagrined at this attempt to inaugurate the 'new regime' to offend and humiliate them during their most devoted Church services."[14]

By approaching the table, the recently emancipated black man was boldly declaring his equality with the white members of the church. The minister refused to give him the Communion elements. In response, the man refused to leave the table. The stalemate was finally broken when General Robert E. Lee "in his usual dignified and self-possessed manner" approached the table and received the elements—ignoring the black man altogether. The rest of the white members followed his example.

The newspaper reported, "By this action of Gen. Lee the services were conducted as if the negro had not been present. It was a grand exhibition of superiority shown by a true Christian and great soldier under the most trying and offensive circumstances."[15]

Many have noted that the Bible does not explicitly forbid slavery—a fact often cited by those who opposed abolition. However, those who read the New Testament thoughtfully will recognize the way it dismantles the social, theological, and even economic values that make slavery possible—particularly the race-based chattel slavery found in America. Paul's command regarding the Lord's Table, for example, forbids the church from separating itself into different groups or classes, and he calls such segregation "sinning against the body and blood of the Lord" (1 Cor. 11:27 NIV).

To share the same table, partake of the same bread, and drink from the same cup is a bold declaration of our equality before God. The Lord's Table, when faithfully and biblically practiced, shatters the heresy of white supremacy. We cannot be sisters and brothers at the table and long remain masters and slaves in the fields. For this reason, those determined to maintain the evil of race-based chattel slavery could not practice the Lord's Supper as commanded in the New Testament. Instead, to avoid the table's society-changing power, they had to pervert it into a tool of inequality, division, and oppression.

The same tendency continues today. A Lord's Table that sees everyone as equal and confronts injustice is still too "provoking and irritating" for some Christians. And churches that are determined to maintain or ignore the unjust systems of the world must still contend with the revolutionary implications of the Lord's Table. This happens in two ways. Either they will ignore the table altogether by removing it from their regular worship, or they will warp the table into a private, individualized sacrament stripped of any social or communal dimensions. By doing so, however, they are no longer partaking of the Lord's Table but the world's.

 READ MORE: **1 Corinthians 11:17–34; Galatians 3:26–28**

EUCHARIST [YOO-KUH-RIST]

NOUN - FROM GREEK MEANING...

~~1. SMALL BREAD AND DRINK~~
~~2. HOLY SNACK~~
~~3. SOMBER MEMORIAL~~
4. THANKSGIVING

19

IF JESUS WAS SERIOUS . . . THEN WE DON'T JUST REMEMBER AT HIS TABLE, WE CELEBRATE.

VARIOUS CHRISTIAN TRADITIONS use different names for the table sacrament of the church. Some call it Communion, others speak about the Lord's Supper, but one of the oldest and most fascinating names is the Eucharist from the Greek word meaning *thanksgiving*. When I first learned this etymology, I was confused. Up to that time, my church experience with the table had always been serious and reflective. The bread and cup memorialized the horrific death of Christ—a moment of unimaginable pain and grief and, as Jesus Himself called it, "the hour when darkness reigned" (Luke 22:53). As a result, in my church tradition, coming to the table on the first Sunday of every month was always somber and never celebratory.

So, why did the earliest Christians call the meal *Eucharist*—a word emphasizing gratitude, joy, and celebration? What did they see in the bread and cup that I had not?

Unlike first-century Romans and Jews, the earliest Christians came to see the cross as a symbol of glory rather than one of shame. Through His death, Jesus had disarmed the power of evil, injustice, and death. What the world saw as Jesus' defeat they came to celebrate as His great victory. As a result, sharing the bread and cup became a way for Christians to express gratitude for their redemption from darkness, as well as a way to celebrate their Lord's triumph over the world. That's why early Christians didn't merely "take Communion." Instead, they "celebrated the Eucharist."

Seeing the table as a symbol of victory, not just death, and taking the bread and cup as an act of gratitude, not merely one of memorial, also carries an unexpected power for believers. Over time, as we celebrate the Eucharist week after week, it can transform our understanding of our own struggles and defeats. Although we may approach the meal at times when it feels as if darkness reigns, Christ's table shows us the power of God to redeem all things and turn our mourning into gladness. As Henri Nouwen wrote:

> The word "Eucharist" means literally "act of
> thanksgiving." To celebrate the Eucharist and to

live a Eucharistic life has everything to do with gratitude. Living Eucharistically is living life as a gift, a gift for which one is grateful. But gratitude is not the most obvious response to life, certainly not when we experience life as a series of losses! Still, the great mystery we celebrate in the Eucharist and live in a Eucharistic life is precisely that through mourning our losses we come to know life as a gift.[16]

READ MORE: John 6:31–40; Colossians 2:13–15

HOSPITALITY = HEALING

"A HOME FOR STRANGERS"

EMERGENCY

WELCOME

20 IF JESUS WAS SERIOUS . . . THEN HIS TABLE IS WHERE THE WOUNDED FIND HEALING.

WHILE RECLINING AT THE TABLE in Matthew's house, enjoying His dinner with the scum of the earth, Jesus noticed the Pharisees had arrived. These religious leaders, masters of image management and experts in social demographics, peered through Matthew's gate at the festivities in the courtyard. Imagine what they saw. A lavish house, a large table filled with food and drink, the courtyard stirring with obnoxious people dancing, smoking, and laughing—behaving the way people do when good wine is abundant. And right in the middle of the revelry was Jesus, the notorious rabbi, reclining at the table and enjoying the party.

The Pharisees were appalled. Calling one of Jesus' disciples to the gate, they inquired with a disgusted tone, "Why does your teacher eat with tax collectors and sinners?" But it was not a disciple who replied. Jesus found the question important enough to answer it Himself. "It is not the healthy who need a doctor, but the sick," He said (Matt. 9:11–12 NIV). The Pharisees saw a rabbi defiling Himself among sinners who were the enemies of God, but with His response, Jesus was trying to open their eyes to see something more. Not a rabbi among sinners, but a doctor healing the sick. Somehow, by simply sharing a table with Matthew and his ungodly friends, Jesus was bringing healing.

The English word *hospitality* originates from the same Latin root as the word "hospital." A hospital is literally a "home for strangers." Of course, it has come to mean a place of healing. There is a link between being welcomed and being healed, and the link is more than just etymological.

When we are loved and accepted for who we really are and welcomed into the life of another person without conditions, it brings healing to our souls. That is what Jesus did by sharing His table with sinners. And it is what His table still does when the church welcomes imperfect, even scandalous people to it.

The love of the world is always conditional. Every corner of our culture and every advertisement we encounter reminds us that our significance and acceptability are rooted in what we achieve, what we have, what we do, how we look, and how we perform. Our acceptability is always conditional, and every human soul carries the wounds of rejection from not meeting someone's standard. How terrible when that wound is inflicted by a parent, a spouse, a community, or a church. Rejection always leaves a wound—not a visible one, but a cut in our souls whose scar we may carry for the remainder of our lives. It's at Christ's table, as we gather to remember His wounds, that we discover ours are welcomed as well.

READ MORE: Matthew 9:9–13; Luke 22:14–20

ALL CHURCHES ARE SACRAMENTAL

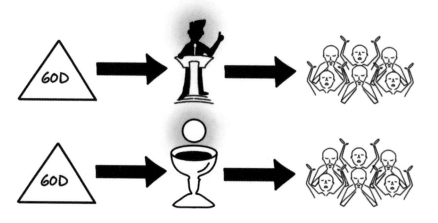

21 | IF JESUS WAS SERIOUS . . . THEN HIS TABLE SHOULD BE MORE REVERED THAN THE PASTOR.

IN SOME CHURCHES, the table is the climax of the community's corporate worship. In these sacramental traditions, the bread and cup are where the people encounter the grace and presence of Christ. Everything else in the gathering—music, prayer, Scripture, and sermon—while meaningful and offering glimpses of glory, are markers along the path as the community ascends together to the summit to meet with God at His table. Sometimes the bread and cup may become so important to a community that they may become idols. The table itself can become an object of worship replacing the One who calls us to it.

To avoid any perception of idolatry, some churches have diminished the role of external symbols, including the Lord's Table, and may even pride themselves on being "non-sacramental." Rather than crosses, icons, or even the table, these churches focus on one's inner connection with God. Revivalist traditions dating back to the eighteenth century, for example, sought to awaken a person's "affections" for God with music and messages targeting the emotions. Rather than emphasizing *external* sacraments, these churches focus on *internal* feelings. As a result, some modern descendants of these traditions have defined the table as an important *ordinance* of the church, but not a sacrament of God's grace and presence. Others, however, have gone much further and marginalized the table or abandoned it altogether.

What these non-sacramental traditions forget, however, is that we are physical, incarnate creatures made to encounter God not merely through our emotions but also with our bodies. When the table is eliminated from our gatherings as the means through which we see, hear, smell, touch, and taste Christ, it creates a deficiency in our worship. We crave a visible, sensory encounter with God and if the table no longer fulfills this function in the church, we will find something else. As Aristotle said, "Nature abhors a vacuum," and so does the church. In my experience, the sacred vacuum once occupied by the table is too often filled by the pastor instead.

We come to expect the presence of Christ and His grace to be encountered through the personality of the person on the platform. They become a sacred object in the eyes of the congregation, and the sermon then becomes the climax of the gathering—the summit everything else must build up to. The awe and reverence some churches exhibit toward the bread and cup are instead projected upon the pastor to the point that in some congregations the line between worshiping Christ and worshiping the pastor becomes blurred.

The effect of this has been seen in many non-sacramental evangelical churches devastated by abusive and immoral leaders, and the consequences are far more than institutional. When people view their pastor sacramentally—as their link to Christ and His grace—very often their faith in God Himself is shattered when the pastor is revealed to be a fraud or even just a fallible human being. Don't misunderstand me—sacramental churches have their problems as well—but worrying that the bread and cup might have an affair with the church secretary isn't one of them.

Maybe the table holds the answer, at least in part, to the pandemic of church leadership scandals we are seeing. Perhaps if we learn to encounter Christ again through His table, then we can take our pastors off their unstable pedestals and see them once again as servants of the church rather than as infallible sacraments.

 READ MORE: Luke 24:13–31; 1 Peter 5:1–5

PART 3

THE FAMILY GATHERING

"Sir," the woman said, "I can see that you are a prophet. Our ancestors worshiped on this mountain, but you Jews claim that the place where we must worship is in Jerusalem."

"Woman," Jesus replied, "believe me, a time is coming when you will worship the Father neither on this mountain nor in Jerusalem. You Samaritans worship what you do not know; we worship what we do know, for salvation is from the Jews. Yet a time is coming and has now come when the true worshipers will worship the Father in the Spirit and in truth, for they are the kind of worshipers the Father seeks. God is spirit, and his worshipers must worship in the Spirit and in truth."

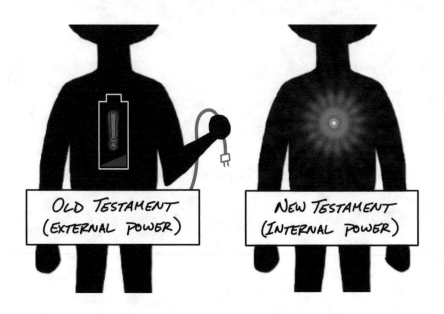

OLD TESTAMENT
(EXTERNAL POWER)

NEW TESTAMENT
(INTERNAL POWER)

22 IF JESUS WAS SERIOUS . . . THEN WORSHIP SHOULD BE MORE THAN A MOUNTAINTOP EXPERIENCE.

WHAT DO YOU EXPECT from a church service? What have you been taught to expect? I often hear church leaders make bold promises about what will happen during their gatherings on Sunday morning. We are told it's where we will "meet God" or that it will be "life transforming." In part, I understand the need for hype and high expectations. It's increasingly difficult to get people to sacrifice their time for anything these days, so churches feel compelled to make big promises about the benefits of giving up your Sunday morning to come to church.

To be clear, I believe we can meet God at church and, of course, a person's life can be transformed by a sermon or song—history is full of examples of both. But there is a significant difference between acknowledging these things *could* happen and promising they *will* happen. The former is a humble recognition of God's power and mystery. The latter is a prideful and downright pagan attempt to control God for our purposes. The truth is, we have no assurances that He will accomplish what we expect through sixty to ninety minutes of singing and a lecture, and I wonder if the promises of some church leaders and our inflated expectations are partly responsible for the disappointment so many have with the church today.

In most cases, I do not think our church gatherings are the problem, but rather what we expect from them. Both church leaders and laity have come to believe these external experiences are the primary vehicle for encountering God and growing in faith. During Jesus' ministry, Jews and Samaritans vigorously disagreed about which mountain was the proper location for worship, but that true worship required climbing a mountain was never questioned. They all agreed that worship and encountering God was an external event. This assumption is what Jesus challenged in His conversation with the Samaritan women in John 4. Rather than emphasize external elements, like mountains, Jesus said true worship is an inner posture of Spirit and truth.

Like the bickering Jews and Samaritans, we fixate upon

the mechanics of worship and often disagree strongly over external issues like style of music, decor, schedule, and location. All of these fights, however, assume worship is an event; a mountain we climb to experience God. Fundamentally, this mountain view is an old covenant idea. Moses, for example, climbed Mount Sinai to enter God's presence and glory. Later, God's people built a temple on Mount Zion in Jerusalem as the abode of God's glory and the centerpiece of their worship. It's worth remembering, however, that as glorious as Moses's encounter with the Lord was on the mountain, the moment he descended, the glory started to fade. The transformation Moses experienced, while real, was only temporary.

In the New Testament, Jesus and His apostles do not copy the old covenant's model of mountains, temples, and external events. Instead, their focus is on a mysterious communion with God made possible through the indwelling presence of His Holy Spirit. Contrasting the fading glory that Moses experienced on the mountain, Paul says that we are being transformed "from one degree of glory to another" (1 Cor. 3:18). It is an ever-increasing change, and this power is not conducted through a sermon, or song, or service. It comes from the Spirit. In other words, for those who belong to the new covenant in Christ, God and His transforming glory are no longer found through *external* events, but through *internal* communion. Worship isn't about climbing mountains, but about retreating into communion through prayer.

This truth should profoundly change our expectations for our church gatherings. It means we don't *find* communion with God by attending a worship event. Instead, we *express* our communion with God by attending a worship event. Sunday morning is when Christians who have been living with God all week gather to outwardly express that reality together and to encourage those for whom it's been a struggle. And rather than expecting the preacher or musicians to mediate God's presence to us each weekend, that responsibility belongs rightfully to the Holy Spirit who abides with us every day and everywhere we go. Maybe if we expected more of God's Spirit Monday through Saturday, we might be content to expect less from our gathering on Sunday and, maybe, we'd argue less with one another about the details.

 READ MORE: Exodus 34:29–35; 2 Corinthians 3:12–18

CONSUMER CHRISTIANITY

TRUE CHRISTIANITY

WHAT I GET

WORSHIP R.O.I.

WHAT I GIVE

23 IF JESUS WAS SERIOUS . . . THEN OUR WORSHIP WON'T ALWAYS BE PRACTICAL.

SIR ALEC GUINNESS was one of Britain's most celebrated actors. I first knew him as Obi-Wan Kenobi in the original Star Wars trilogy. Later, I discovered his earlier films like *The Bridge on the River Kwai*, which remains among my favorites. In his autobiography, Guinness described an odd event that occurred while he was walking through London. He wrote: "I was walking up Kingsway in the middle of an afternoon when an impulse compelled me to start running. With joy in my heart, and in a state of excitement, I ran until I reached the little church there which I had never entered before; I knelt; caught my breath, and for ten minutes was lost to the world."[17]

This spontaneous sprint into a church happened not long after Guinness completed his journey from atheism to faith in Christ. He was at a loss to explain exactly what compelled him to kneel in the church and present himself before God. Guinness finally concluded that it was a "rather nonsensical gesture of love."[18] That may be the best definition of worship I have ever found.

We live in an age of Christian pragmatism. The influence of business and industry has seeped into the church and convinced many that the church ought to adopt the methods and metrics of the marketplace. Likewise, in many places, the Sunday worship gathering is designed with customer feedback in mind. *How many came? Did they like the music? Was the sermon helpful enough? How much did they give?* Of course, it's not just church leaders who are constrained by pragmatism. Many church members approach worship with a similar calculation. *Did I receive enough from the church to justify giving up my Sunday morning?*

These calculations betray the reason we worship. We do not gather on Sunday because it will measurably improve our lives, families, or careers. And churches that engineer their services to increase institutional growth are at risk of allowing logistics to eclipse love. Don't get me wrong, practical considerations have their place, but when it overshadows everything else—even our worship—it's an indication that we've succumbed to pagan values rather than Christian ones. As C. S.

Lewis noted in *The Magician's Nephew*, "I expect most witches are like that. They are not interested in things or people unless they can use them; they are terribly practical."[19]

Alec Guinness had it right—if we've encountered the holy, mysterious, and infinitely loving God then there will be things about our communion with Him that defy usefulness and that are utterly nonsensical. This is true of love even on a human level. There is nothing practical about presenting my wife with a bundle of dying plants severed from their roots, but she's delighted when I give her flowers. And I am delighted by her delight. Likewise, there may have been no practical reason for Jesus to turn water into wine at a wedding, or for God to put "every beautiful tree" in the garden for Adam and Eve to enjoy, or for Him to adopt us into His family and lavish His love upon us. Maybe these were all simply expressions of His nonsensical love.

And maybe that's what worship is. It's what happens when God's delight in us inspires our delight in Him, sparking an endless loop of joy between Creator and creature, between Lover and beloved. That seems beyond any organizational metric or customer feedback survey. And if our primary goal for Sunday worship is self-improvement or institutional growth, then we should admit we aren't really there to worship God at all, but to *use* Him. And if our worship is always driven by pragmatism, let's confess that it isn't really worship. It is witchcraft.

 READ MORE: **John 2:1–11; Psalm 27:1–4**

Q: According to Hebrews 10, we should gather regularly in order to do what?

A: LEARN

B. SERVE

C: WORSHIP

GOD

D: ENCOURAGE

A: D: ENCOURAGE ONE ANOTHER.

24 IF JESUS WAS SERIOUS . . .
THEN WE MUST NOT GIVE UP
MEETING TOGETHER.

DURING THE COVID-19 PANDEMIC, many Christians were unable to meet together. According to many health experts, a large, indoor gathering with singing is ideal for a "super-spreader" event and posed an especially high risk for the elderly and those with underlying health problems. But they're not the only ones avoiding church meetings. In a very unscientific poll of my Twitter followers during the pandemic, I asked how many were engaging with their church community either online or in person. The results were evenly split, but a significant number—about 25 percent—admitted they had disengaged completely. With the distribution of the vaccine, and with the pandemic receding, most expected church attendance to rebound. But in some places it hasn't.

Increasingly, I'm hearing Christians question the value of their church's Sunday gathering, and the move to online streaming services during the pandemic only accelerated the discontent. I wonder if earlier generations were equally frustrated with church gatherings but carried a greater sense of duty to persevere. Or perhaps there was simply greater social pressure to attend church, which in many communities has since disappeared. Regardless of the cause, if we are serious about our faith but struggling with attending church, then at some point we must wrestle with what Scripture says about it.

The writer of Hebrews clearly instructs believers to "not give up meeting together" (Heb. 10:25 NIV), but we often overlook the reason we're supposed to meet together. The writer of the letter could have listed any number of reasons for gathering—to offer our worship to God, to learn sound doctrine from our teachers, to be equipped for our mission as Christ's disciples. But he lists none of these. Instead, the author of Hebrews offers a more basic, human, and pastoral reason. We are to meet regularly to encourage "one another."

I wonder if the growing dissatisfaction with church gatherings—both physical and virtual—is rooted in their failure to accomplish this most important function. They may be informative with profound preaching. They may be entertaining with riveting music. But those are qualities easily accomplished from a stage or screen. The kind of faith-building encouragement commanded in Hebrews, however, is personal, relational, and reciprocal. It's not accomplished by passively sitting in a theater seat watching a performance. This kind of encouragement requires us to be fully present and engaged. It's the arm-around-a-shoulder, praying-together-with-tears, let-me-help-you-carry-that-burden kind of gathering. It's the kind where no one is invisible and everyone is seen.

In our rapidly changing and turbulent society, that kind of gathering is needed now more than ever, but it's also more difficult to find as we are more isolated than previous generations because of technology and social divisions. But Jesus also said that when even just two or three gather in His name, "there am I among them"(Matt. 18:20). He doesn't promise to be in front of us on a platform or watching us on a live feed. He promises to be *with* us, just as we are with each other. This means we may encounter Him just as easily, and maybe more so, in a small gathering than in a large one. And because He is with us, as we meet with even just a few Christian brothers or sisters we can know that the arm we place on a shoulder, or the tear we shed in prayer, or the hand that lifts our burden, will be Christ's own.

 READ MORE: Hebrews 10:23–25; Matthew 18:15–18

25   IF JESUS WAS SERIOUS . . . THEN WE GATHER TO SEE THROUGH ONE ANOTHER'S EYES.

THE FACT THAT JOHN THE BAPTIST struggled with doubt should be a great comfort to us. Consider John's spiritual credentials. His birth had been a miracle foretold by an angel. He grew to be a mighty prophet "strong in spirit" (Luke 1:80). Crowds followed him; kings feared him. It was John who first recognized Jesus' divine identity. He leaped in his mother's womb at the sound of Mary's voice while she was pregnant with Jesus. John proclaimed to the crowds along the riverbank, "Behold, the

Lamb of God, who takes away the sins of the world!" (John 1:29). And he baptized Jesus when the voice of the Father declared, "This is my beloved Son" (Matt. 3:17).

Despite experiencing all of this, when his circumstances turned dark and he was rotting in King Herod's dungeon, doubts haunted John's faith. Everything he could see made him question God's goodness and Jesus' identity. *If Jesus really is the one, why am I in prison? If Jesus really is the one, why is He allowing an evil and illegitimate king to get away with injustice? If Jesus really is the one, why am I about to lose my life?*

Plagued by these questions, John finally sent his friends to Jesus to ask him directly, "Are you the one who is to come, or should we look for another?" It's important to see that Jesus did not condemn John for doubting. He did not say, "John, of all people you should know better. After all you've seen and experienced, how could you possibly doubt Me?" Instead, Jesus showed compassion. He understood John's struggles and the horrible circumstances that caused them. Rather than condemning John's doubts, Jesus responded by encouraging his faith. He said to John's friends, "Go and tell John what you have seen" (see Luke 7:18–23).

Jesus knew that in Herod's dungeon John's vision was severely limited. He saw only darkness, evil, and injustice. Jesus sent John's friends to him with a different vision; they were to be John's eyes for him. They were to help him see what he could no longer see. Through their report, John would be given a glimpse of the beauty, power, and light of God that still shined beyond his present darkness.

Sometimes our circumstances make us blind to God and

we become vulnerable to doubts and fears. In such times we need our friends, we need our community, we need the church. When our world is hidden in darkness and we can no longer see the goodness of God, that is when we must borrow the eyes of another. That is what it means for the church to gather and encourage one another. If we, like John's friends, have seen the power and grace of Christ, we must not withhold that news from our sister or brother who sits in darkness and doubt. Our testimony can be the eyes through which they catch a glimpse of God again and receive the strength to journey on.

As we gather as a church each week, some will be like John in a dungeon of misery and doubt. Others, like John's friends, will have been with Jesus and seen the promised land. On any given Sunday, those of us with vision are to become the eyes of those who are blind, knowing the next week we may be in the dungeon needing to borrow the eyes of our brother on the mountaintop.

 READ MORE: Luke 7:18–23; Hebrews 10:23–25

26 IF JESUS WAS SERIOUS . . . THEN THE CHURCH GATHERS FOR COMMUNITY, NOT FOR A CONCERT.

MANY HAVE COME TO SEE the church primarily as an event rather than as a community. It is something they *attend* rather than something they *are*. It's like professional sports except the ball is replaced with a Bible. It's like a Broadway production except the performer is a pastor rather than a tenor. It's like a rock concert except the feeling of euphoria is attributed to the Spirit rather than the secondhand smoke.

What all of these experiences share in common is the general passivity of the audience. They gather to be entertained, informed, or amused by the performers on the stage or the field. Very little is expected of those gathered other than a financial contribution via ticket or tithe. Cheers or applause is welcomed, but everyone knows the audience is not essential to the gathering. The show could just as easily go on without them.

Sadly, this consumer ethic of passive amusement has deeply influenced much of the modern church and its gatherings. As Sally Morganthaler writes:

> *We are not producing worshipers in this country. Rather, we are producing a generation of spectators, religious onlookers lacking, in many cases, any memory of a true encounter with God, deprived of both the tangible sense of God's presence and the supernatural relationship their inmost spirits crave.*[20]

Of course, biblically speaking, church is not an event; it's a community. The church is the assembly of women, men, and children redeemed by Christ, filled with His Spirit, and living in communion with Him and each other in a way that reveals to the world the invading reality of God's kingdom. That kind of community requires us to be full participants and not merely spectators.

Remember, Jesus did not say where two or three are gathered I will stand before them. He said, "I will be in the midst of them." The presence of God is revealed in the *relationships* between His people, not on a stage in front of them.

 READ MORE: Matthew 18:15–18; Colossians 3:12–17

FLIGHT 143
HAS LANDED!

AS FLIGHT 143 REDUCED THRUST, AIR-FLOW OVER THE WING SLOWED CAUSING THE PRESSURE DIFFERENCE ABOVE AND BELOW THE WING TO NARROW RESULTING IN A LOSS OF LIFT. DRAG FROM AIR RESISTANCE THEN...

PREACHING VS. TEACHING

27 IF JESUS WAS SERIOUS . . . THEN ONLY THE MATURE SHOULD TEACH, BUT ANYONE CAN PREACH.

RATATOUILLE **IS ONE OF MY FAVORITE MOVIES.** It's about a rat named Remy who refuses to eat garbage like the rest of his family. Instead, he prefers the delicate interplay of flavors found in fine cuisine. When Remy discovers his own hidden talent for French cooking, no one believes a rat can become a great chef. Still, he finds inspiration in the motto of his mentor: "Anyone can cook!"

Likewise, some of us have come to believe that preaching

is the responsibility of a few educated and gifted people within the church. We think preaching requires theological education and deep biblical insight, a proficiency of knowledge most of us will never acquire. This is because we have misunderstood what preaching really means. What we find in the New Testament, however, is that anyone can preach.

For example, Jesus sent His disciples out into the villages of Judea to "preach" the kingdom of God when they were still confused about the most basic facts. Later in the gospel accounts, these same men would display their profound ignorance about the nature of God, His kingdom, Jesus' mission, and even Jesus' identity. And yet, they were actively preaching throughout the land. In most of our churches, these men wouldn't be allowed near a Sunday school class let alone a pulpit. So why did Jesus command them to "preach the kingdom"?

The problem is that we confuse *teaching* with *preaching*. Teaching requires proficiency with a set of knowledge; it requires comprehension. Jesus doesn't tell His disciples to "teach" until *after* His resurrection when they finally understood his identity and mission. Preaching, on the other hand, simply means "to proclaim" or "to announce." Preaching requires one to have experienced what is being proclaimed, but it doesn't mean you completely understand it.

For example, *preaching* is announcing that flight 143 from Cincinnati has arrived. *Teaching* is explaining the aerodynamic forces of drag, lift, and thrust that allowed the airplane to land. Not everyone possesses the knowledge to teach, but anyone with a genuine experience of God's kingdom can preach.

If you have a story of encountering Christ, His power, and His kingdom then you are qualified to preach, even if you can't fully explain the experience. Far too many of God's people neglect this calling because we have incorrectly made it the domain of trained experts, and this has profoundly warped our church gatherings into a time when nearly everyone is silent and only one person—the one possessing the most knowledge—is permitted to speak.

Don't misunderstand me. Teaching is an important aspect of the church's calling, and we should not neglect it. But when only one person is expected to arrive to the gathering with something to share, what are we communicating about the value of everyone else? Proclaiming the present reality of God's kingdom—announcing how we have seen and experienced His love, power, and mercy—is not the domain of the elite or the educated. It is the calling of every one of Christ's people. Anyone can preach.

 READ MORE: Matthew 10:5–10; Acts 1:6–8

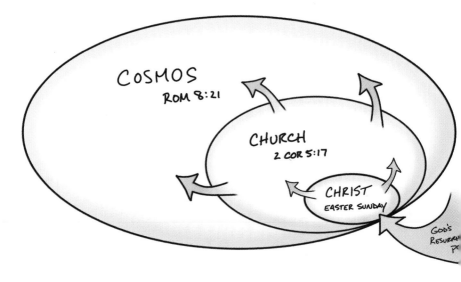

28 IF JESUS WAS SERIOUS . . . THEN WHY DO WE WORSHIP ON SUNDAY?

WHY DOES THE CHURCH WORSHIP on Sunday? You may know the Sunday school answer—because Jesus rose from the dead on a Sunday. That is certainly true, but have you ever wondered *why* Jesus rose from the dead on a Sunday?

It goes back to the ancient biblical story of creation in Genesis 1. The first day of creation was a Sunday, and God rested on the last day of the week—Saturday (from which the Israelites based their own practice of Sabbath rest on Saturday).

Jesus was raised to life on a Sunday because His resurrection was the beginning of the new creation. Easter was the start of God "making all things new" in Christ. As the apostle Paul says in 1 Corinthians 15, resurrection is the "firstfruits" of God's redemption—the start of something that will extend far beyond an empty tomb in Jerusalem.

We worship on Sunday not merely to acknowledge the reality of Jesus' resurrection. We worship on Sunday not simply to celebrate our own redemption and access to eternal life through the cross and empty tomb. We worship on Sunday because through Christ we have become a new creation (2 Cor. 5:17), and we have become a people of the new creation. The community of the church is supposed to be a sign to the world of the new reality that has begun—one in which ethnic and social divisions are mended, hatred is undone by love, and evil is overcome by good.

Like the creation account in Genesis, which began but did not end on the first Sunday, God's re-creation began on Easter Sunday and continues to unfold even now. This power touched our lives when were made new in Christ, and the day is approaching when the resurrection power of Christ will fill every corner of the cosmos until "the creation itself will be set free from its bondage to corruption and obtain the freedom of the glory of the children of God" (Rom. 8:21).

So, the day we gather as a church isn't merely about convenience, and the tradition of gathering on Sunday wasn't a random decision made centuries ago that we have blindly continued. There is a deep meaning and a profound symbolism behind the worship of Christians on Sunday stretching back to the opening words of the Bible. Sunday is about creation and new creation, and it captures the essence of God's mission, and ours, to make all things new.

 READ MORE: **1 Corinthians 15:20–26; Revelation 21:3–5**

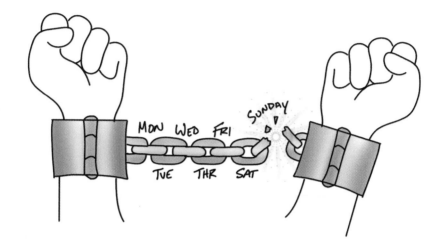

29 IF JESUS WAS SERIOUS . . . THEN WHY DOESN'T THE CHURCH WORSHIP ON SATURDAY?

FOR THOUSANDS OF YEARS, Jews have refrained from working on the last day of the week in obedience to God's command in the Old Testament. Christians, with a few exceptions, have not followed this tradition and instead made Sunday—the first day of the week—their time for worship and rest. What's behind this change and why don't we still worship and rest on Saturday?

To understand the move from Saturday to Sunday, we first

have to expand our understanding of the Sabbath in the Old Testament. Most root their knowledge of the Sabbath in the creation story in Genesis where the Lord created the world in six days and rested on the seventh. If six days of work was good enough for God, the saying goes, it should be enough for us. What often gets overlooked, however, is who wrote Genesis and for whom. Tradition tells us that Moses composed the first five books of the Hebrew Bible, and Genesis was written for the Israelites who had just been rescued from slavery in Egypt. This detail is critical to understanding God's intent for the Sabbath rest.

In Deuteronomy 5, for example, Moses directly links the command to rest from work with the Lord's rescue of His people from slavery. While in bondage in Egypt the Israelites never got a day off from work. To remember God's deliverance and their new status as a free people, the Israelites were to rest from all of their work every Saturday, which their ancestors in Egypt could never do, and they were to extend this same dignity to all of their servants, to immigrants, and even to their animals. It appears Moses then used his creation narrative in Genesis to reiterate and reinforce this principle. At its core, Sabbath is about freedom from bondage, not merely rest from activity.

Once we see the link between Sabbath and slavery, Jesus' controversial actions on the Sabbath also begin to make sense. He was repeatedly criticized by religious leaders for "working" on Saturday because He continued to heal many people. "There are six days in which work ought to be done," said one angry synagogue ruler. "Come on those days to be healed, and not on the Sabbath day." The religious elites were narrowly focused on the command to not work, but Jesus was focused on the *reason* for not working. "You hypocrites!" Jesus shot back. "Ought not this woman, a daughter of Abraham whom Satan bound for eighteen years, be loosed from this bond on the Sabbath day?" (see Luke 13:14–16). He understood that the Sabbath itself was a sign of freedom from bondage, and there was no real Sabbath rest for those still enslaved by disease. By healing, Jesus was *fulfilling* the meaning of the Sabbath, not violating it.

So, what does this have to do with the move from Saturday to Sunday worship? The Sabbath commandment in the Old Testament, like so many others, was a sign pointing to the ultimate deliverance from all evil that God would accomplish for all of creation through His Son. The earliest Christians recognized this cosmic deliverance was won for us when Jesus conquered death on Easter Sunday. Through the resurrection, Christ has inaugurated the final and ultimate rest by setting us free from slavery to sin, evil, and death.

Therefore, Christians have commemorated the world's freedom and our deliverance on Sunday—the day our slavery was ended. And the way we now practice Sabbath isn't merely resting from work one day a week. Instead, like Jesus, we continue to seek the deliverance of all people from every form of slavery—whether idolatry, evil, sin, injustice, sickness, or death. For the Christian, the Sabbath isn't just a day of rest or worship; it's a day for mission and justice.

 READ MORE: Deuteronomy 5:12–15; Luke 13:10–17

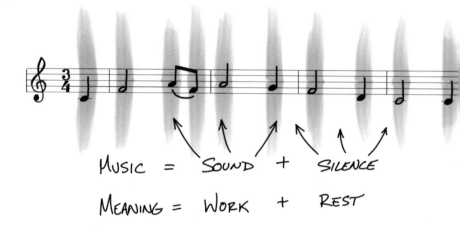

MUSIC = SOUND + SILENCE

MEANING = WORK + REST

30 IF JESUS WAS SERIOUS . . . THEN THE CHURCH SHOULD PRACTICE A RHYTHM OF REST.

COLONEL WILLIAM POGUE was the first American to go on strike in space. Midway through his eighty-four-day mission in 1974, Col. Pogue and the other astronauts onboard the Skylab space station requested an adjustment to their work schedule for more rest. "We had been over-scheduled," Pogue said. "We were just hustling the whole day. The work could be tiresome and tedious, though the view was spectacular." Ground control rejected their request. The work was too important, they said, and time was limited. Some worried the astronauts' request for time off was an indication of depression or other illness from their long exposure to weightlessness. Pogue said no one was sick or anxious. They just wanted more time to look out the window and think, he said.

Eventually, the disagreement between the astronauts and controllers became so intense the astronauts went on strike. Finally, a compromise was reached that gave the crew more time to rest during the remaining six weeks of the flight. Pogue later wrote that having more time to look out the window at the sun and earth below also made him reflect more about himself, his crew, and their "human situation, instead of trying to operate like a machine."[21]

Like Col. Pogue and his crew, we need to set aside time from our work—including church work—to gaze out the capsule window and contemplate our lives and calling from a cosmic perspective. This is what the church's Sunday worship is for. It provides perspective. At their best, the songs, sacraments, and sermons are designed to raise our sights to heavenly beauties, to reconsider our lives and our world from God's point of view, and then prepare us to reenter the atmosphere of the ordinary with a renewed sense of meaning and communion with God.

Some churches, however, operate more like ground control by utilizing Sunday to recruit more people to do more work. The work is too important, church leaders say, and time is too limited. There's no time for rest. There's no time in our church service for silence. We can't slow down to reflect or meditate—we have things to accomplish in these seventy-five minutes together. Goodness, in many of our churches there isn't even time for prayer or Communion anymore. Rather than lifting our eyes to the horizon, some church gatherings are designed to keep our noses to the grindstone.

Of course, this is not an either/or issue. Like the astronauts on the space station, we do have important work to accomplish, and the church's mission can sometimes be tiresome and tedious. And our church leaders are there to equip and guide us in this calling both individually and together. But we are not machines, and God has not redeemed us merely to put us to work. That's why we need a regular rhythm of work and rest, of mission and meditation, in order to see ourselves, our work, our church, and our Lord from the right perspective.

 READ MORE: Mark 2:23–28; Matthew 11:28–30

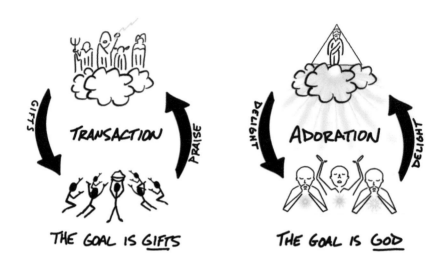

THE GOAL IS <u>GIFTS</u>

THE GOAL IS <u>GOD</u>

31 IF JESUS WAS SERIOUS . . . THEN TRUE WORSHIP IS NEVER TRANSACTIONAL.

ALMOST EVERY ANCIENT creation myth says that humans were created to serve the gods. We were needed to build the gods' temples, to provide food to the gods through our sacrifices, and to appease the gods' anger with our prayers and worship. Pagan mythologies said our human purpose was to be the gods' slaves.

This pagan vision of life and worship is turned upside down by what God reveals about Himself in the Hebrew Scriptures. Unlike the gods of Babylon, Egypt, or Rome, the God of

Israel did not need to be fed, clothed, or housed by people. "If I were hungry, I would not tell you," He said, "for the world and its fullness are mine" (Ps. 50:12). And the Bible is clear that God does not live in a temple built by people but has made the whole universe His dwelling place (Isa. 66:1). In other words, Israel's God did not *need* us. He does not need your service, offerings, praise, prayers, *or your Sunday morning.*

So if God did not create us to serve Him, and if there is nothing we can properly offer to Him, what is the point of our worship? Within this question, we discover the problem. Because of our consumer mindset, we assume that worship must have a concrete outcome; some practical purpose that measurably benefits either us or God. In this formulation—which is the hallmark of paganism—worship is a means to an end; it is a transaction in which we offer to the deity what he needs (praise, prayers, sacrifices) and in response, we expect to receive what we need (blessing, protection, wealth, etc.).

Here's a simple, but useful, example. Back in 2010, Steve Johnson was a wide receiver for the Buffalo Bills. In an overtime playoff game against the Pittsburgh Steelers, the Bills lost when Johnson dropped a pass in the end zone. After the game, Johnson tweeted: *"I praise you 24/7!!! And this is how you do me!!! You expect me to learn from this??? How??? I'll never forget this!! Ever!!"*[22] I generally avoid getting my theology from Twitter, and we certainly should not draw conclusions about Johnson from a single social media outburst. That being said, his tweet perfectly captures a transactional understanding of worship. He offered God his praise 24/7, and in exchange he expected divine help catching footballs. Steve Johnson had kept his end of the deal but felt God had failed to uphold his.

This is not Christianity. It is paganism. And it is not biblical worship. It's an attempt to control God with offerings, sacrifices, and incantations.

Properly understood, true Christian worship is never transactional. God delights in our praises, but He does not *need* them. And in worship, we may experience grace and illumination—but these are not guaranteed. Rather than seeing worship as a means to an end, Christian faith understands God to be an end in Himself. As David declares: "One thing have I asked of the LORD, that will I seek after: that I may dwell in the house of the LORD all the days of my life, to gaze upon the beauty of the LORD" (Ps. 27:4). We gather to worship for no more practical reason than to adore our Creator and Redeemer, and in the process we discover something equally impractical—that He adores us as well.

 READ MORE: Psalm 27:1–4; Psalm 50:7–15

PS. 27:4

32 IF JESUS WAS SERIOUS . . . THEN WORSHIP IS ABOUT SEEING GOD'S INTRINSIC VALUE, NOT HIS USEFULNESS.

WHEN READING THE GOSPELS, it's worth paying attention to what gets people upset. For example, King Herod gets upset when he hears a new king has been born. The religious leaders get upset when they see Jesus sharing a table with sinners. Jesus gets upset when He sees merchants buying and selling in the temple courtyard. And Jesus' disciples get upset when a woman poured a flask of expensive ointment on Jesus' feet. This last event, recorded in Mark 14, carries an important lesson for us about the nature of worship.

The disciples objected to the woman's behavior because they saw it as reckless and impractical. "Why was this ointment wasted?" they said. "It could have been sold for more than three hundred denarii and given to the poor" (Mark 14:4–5). They were so outraged by her wastefulness that they began scolding her. In their view, she was guilty of extravagance and disregard for the practical needs of others. She was either selfish, foolish, or both.

Jesus, however, saw things very differently and immediately came to the woman's defense. "Leave her alone. Why do you trouble her?" He said. "She has done a beautiful thing to me" (Mark 14:6).

What His disciples saw as wasteful, Jesus saw as beautiful. What they interpreted as selfish, Jesus received as worship. The woman had poured out her most precious possession at Jesus' feet to honor Him. He understood her intent and therefore did not interpret her actions through a lens of practicality. And rather than rebuking her, Jesus praises her. "Truly, I say to you, wherever the gospel is proclaimed in the whole world, what she has done will be told in memory of her" (Mark 14:9).

Real love sees the intrinsic value of that which it adores rather than its transactional value. The disciples saw only the ointment's transactional value—what it could be exchanged for and how it could achieve some practical purpose. Jesus, on the other hand, recognized the woman poured out the precious commodity as an expression of her love. She saw Jesus' intrinsic value, and He affirmed her for it. This is what we, like the first disciples, often miss about worship.

The word *worship* means "to ascribe worth." Unlike religions fueled by superstition or fear, true Christian faith does not worship God with a practical goal in mind. It is not transactional. It is not useful. Worship is an impractical and beautiful act of adoration that flows from a heart transfixed by the beauty of God. That is why Jesus celebrates the woman in Mark 14 and the disciples rebuke her. She was worshiping beautifully, but they could only think of worship transactionally.

 READ MORE: Mark 14:3–9; Psalm 96:1–9

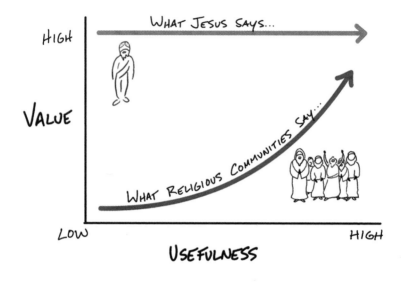

High

Value

Low

What Jesus says...

What Religious Communities say...

Low   High

Usefulness

33 IF JESUS WAS SERIOUS . . . THEN COLLECTIVE WORSHIP IS INSEPARABLE FROM COLLECTIVE JUSTICE.

WHEN A WOMAN POURED very expensive ointment on Jesus in Mark 14, His disciples were outraged at her wastefulness. Unlike Jesus, they were incapable of seeing past the impracticality of her actions to affirm the beauty of her worship. Like the disciples, many of us have difficulty seeing beyond the practical. Our consumer society has formed us to associate value with usefulness, and when something is no longer useful we do not hesitate to throw it away and acquire something else.

That's why the church's worship gatherings should be full of beauty, art, and all sorts of impractical things. They serve to counteract the utilitarian impulse of our culture and remind us that the most important things in the world—God and people—do not exist to be used but to be adored. The great danger of practical, transactional worship is that it shapes us to see God as a mere device, a disposable product. And the way we see God invariably determines how we see those created in His image. If the church's worship communicates, directly or indirectly, that the Creator exists to be used, we shouldn't be surprised to find an indifference among Christians toward people we have determined aren't useful either.

Thankfully, more Christians today are recognizing the reality of oppression and injustice in our world, and our call as God's people to address it. But if we want our world to value orphans, the poor, the trafficked, and the hungry, and if we want to awaken our society to the value of every human life no matter how small, or old, or broken, or different, then we must confront the utilitarian ethic that enslaves us all. We do that by learning to value what is not useful. We do that by cultivating beauty in our worship. Beauty is the prelude for justice, and justice is true worship.

In Isaiah 58, the Lord flatly rejected the worship offered by His people. Their festivals, fasts, and prayers were done transactionally—to achieve God's blessing and favor. At the same time, the people neglected and abused those whom they saw as useless—the homeless, the hungry, and the poor. Pragmatism had infected their worship just as injustice had infected the land. The two always go together. That is why God tells His people to honor the poor, set free the oppressed, and show dignity to those the world calls useless, and "then you shall call, and the LORD will answer; you shall cry, and he will say, 'Here I am'" (Isa. 58:9).

Mark Labberton sees the same danger today. "According to the narrative of Scripture, the very heart of how we show and distinguish true worship from false worship is apparent in how we respond to the poor, the oppressed, the neglected and the forgotten. As of now, I do not see this theme troubling the waters of worship in the American church. . . . Justice and mercy are intrinsic to God and therefore intrinsic to the worship of God."[23]

 READ MORE: Mark 14:3–9; Isaiah 58:1–10

WAR

HOW THE WORLD FIGHTS

WORSHIP

HOW THE CHURCH FIGHTS

34 IF JESUS WAS SERIOUS . . . THEN BEAUTIFUL WORSHIP IS HOW THE CHURCH DEFIES THE WORLD.

MORE THAN TEN THOUSAND PEOPLE were killed during the siege of Sarajevo from 1992 to 1995. Vedran Smailović, the lead cellist in the Sarajevo opera, lived through the carnage and felt powerless to stop it until May 28, 1992. That's when he put on his tuxedo, carried his cello and a chair into the street, sat down in a bomb crater in his neighborhood, and began to play his music. At the same location the previous day, twenty-two people were killed while waiting in line at one of the only working bakeries in the city. Overcome by the horrors of the scene, Smailović continued to play in the crater for twenty-two days, one day for each victim.

Like so many other wars, it was the innocent people in Sarajevo who suffered the most. They lived under the constant fear of bombs and stray bullets. In some cases, snipers deliberately targeted people as they scurried through the streets searching for food and water. Tired of living in fear and grief, Smailović decided to challenge the ugliness of the war with the beauty of his music. He became known as the "Cellist of Sarajevo." After playing at the bombed bakery, he took his cello to cemeteries, he played atop the rubble of fallen buildings, and even sat down in the midst of sniper-infested streets. Remarkably, he was never shot. It was like the sound of his music was a forcefield of protection; an armor against evil. He became a symbol of hope to the people of Sarajevo, and a reminder to the soldiers destroying the city that another way was possible.

A reporter asked him if he was crazy for playing in a war zone. Smajlović replied, "Why don't you go ask those people if they are not crazy, shelling Sarajevo while I sit here playing my cello?"[24]

His story helps illustrate why Christians worship and why our worship should be marked by inexplicable beauty. The church's impractical worship not only reveals God's character to us and teaches us to value Him and others apart from their usefulness, but our worship also confronts the sinfulness of our world. In war, we see the ultimate expression of ungodly utilitarianism. War is supremely practical. It is the willingness to sacrifice literally everything to achieve a goal. When the tanks of war roll, everything gets crushed beneath their treads, leaving only ugliness behind.

Worship, however, is the opposite of war. It is an act of creation rather than destruction, of order rather than chaos, and beauty rather than ugliness. By playing his cello in the center of war-torn Sarajevo, Smajlović was planting a garden amid the battlefield. He was confronting the sinfulness of man seen in the horrible practicality of war, with the beauty of God seen in the extravagant impracticality of art.

Art is more than a luxury, and beauty is more than an extravagance. When we create art and music, or when we gather to worship with expressions of splendor and adoration, as we do every Sunday, like Smajlović, we are performing an act of defiance. We are creating an oasis of beauty amid the dehumanizing ugliness of our world. We are declaring our refusal to succumb to the brutal practicality of the world, which crushes people in its pursuit of power, wealth, or fame. Instead, our worship is a glimpse forward to the new creation Christ has already begun in our midst where all things will radiate the beauty of the Creator, and where justice will roll down like a mighty river.

 READ MORE: Revelation 21:3–7; Romans 12:14–21

WORSHIPER

PRAYERS
SONGS
RITUALS
SACRIFICES

GODS

THERE ARE NO STRINGS ON ME!

35 IF JESUS WAS SERIOUS . . . THEN TRUE WORSHIP IS ABOUT RELATIONSHIPS, NOT RITUALS.

NO ONE IN THE BIBLE epitomizes worship more than David. He composed nearly half of the psalms, was mocked by some for his enthusiastic singing and dancing before the Lord, and had the goal of building a permanent place for worship in Jerusalem. And yet, David understood worship wasn't primarily about music, or rituals, or temples. For example, after being confronted with his own sin and crying out to God in confession, David said: "For you will not delight in sacrifice, or I would give it; you will not be pleased with a burnt offering. The sacrifices of God are a broken spirit; a broken and contrite heart, O God, you will not despise" (Ps. 51:16–17).

If we recall the strict structures of worship commanded in the Old Testament, David's words appear shocking and even blasphemous—especially coming from Israel's king. Remember, there was a tabernacle—and later a temple—in Jerusalem where sacrifices and offerings were made to God. There were elaborate rituals mediated by priests, and festivals throughout the year established on a set calendar. All of these very precise, liturgical, and formal structures of worship were set up by the Lord Himself through Moses and outlined in the Torah, Israel's Law.

But in Psalm 51, David, Israel's king, dismisses this entire, God-ordained system of sacrifices and rituals—*not* because the system itself was wrong, but because David understood it was always intended to express a deeper reality. He says God does not delight in these external performances and symbols, because what He really desires is our hearts. David recognized that if we do not genuinely *want* God, no amount of singing or sacrifices will make our worship acceptable. This deeper understanding, the ability to see the intent behind the instruments of worship, was rare in the ancient world and remains rare today.

In modern societies, we tend to see God as a machine, and therefore we engage worship as a program or formula. As long as we provide the right inputs (sacrifices, prayers, rituals), then we believe we will get the right outputs (forgiveness, blessings, and euphoria). Premodern societies often saw God like an irrational child given to tantrums when His pacifier is taken away.

Some of us still hold this view. We think sin will trigger His wrath, so we scramble to offer the right sacrifices, say the right prayers, or write a large enough check as a means of putting the pacifier back in His mouth.

These mechanical, patronizing views of God are insulting. They assume all He cares about is sin and all He wants is atonement like some mythical beast from a Greek epic. David, having a deeper communion with the Lord, recognized that rituals, sacrifices, and offerings are not what God ultimately wants, and we cannot control Him with these mechanics of worship. What He desires is *us*. True worship is the expression of a relationship, not merely the performance of a ritual.

 READ MORE: Psalm 51:1–17; John 4:19–24

PART 4

THE FAMILY BUSINESS

When Jesus came to the region of Caesarea Philippi, he asked his disciples, "Who do people say the Son of Man is?"

They replied, "Some say John the Baptist; others say Elijah; and still others, Jeremiah or one of the prophets."

"But what about you?" he asked. "Who do you say I am?"
Simon Peter answered, "You are the Messiah, the Son of the living God."

Jesus replied, "Blessed are you, Simon son of Jonah, for this was not revealed to you by flesh and blood, but by my Father in heaven. And I tell you that you are Peter, and on this rock I will build my church, and the gates of Hades will not overcome it. I will give you the keys of the kingdom of heaven; whatever you bind on earth will be bound in heaven, and whatever you loose on earth will be loosed in heaven."

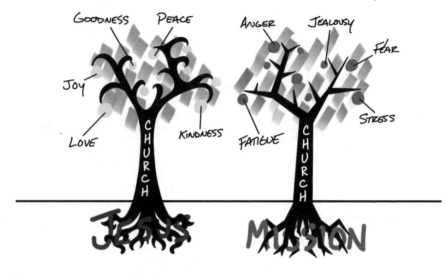

36 | IF JESUS WAS SERIOUS . . . THEN THE FOUNDATION OF THE CHURCH IS JESUS HIMSELF, NOT OUR MISSION.

WHAT IS THE MOST IMPORTANT THING in a church? What binds a Christian community together? What is the irreducible, irreplaceable foundation upon which everything else depends?

In 1 Corinthians 3, the apostle Paul uses the extended metaphor of a temple under construction to describe the community of believers in Corinth. In an unusual bit of boasting, Paul calls himself "a skilled master builder" who laid the foundation of this temple upon which others are now building. This is a reference to Paul being the first person to bring the message of Jesus to the city of Corinth. He goes on, "For no one can lay a foundation other than that which is laid, which is Jesus Christ" (1 Cor. 3:11). In his letter to the church in Ephesus, Paul used a similar metaphor and once again compared the church to a temple under construction. In Ephesians 2, he identified Christ Jesus as "the cornerstone, in whom the whole structure, being joined together, grows into a holy temple in the Lord" (Eph. 2:20–21).

In both letters, Paul is unambiguous—Jesus Christ Himself is the irreducible, irreplaceable foundation of the church. At first, this may not strike you as surprising, but upon closer inspection, it profoundly challenges many of our modern assumptions. Here's why—many churches today have been deeply influenced by corporate business values. The best run, most effective organizations in our society are for-profit enterprises, and for the last fifty years, many churches have been eager to copy their strategies. On the surface, this mimicry of the marketplace appears wise. If corporations have proven strategies for selling coffee and chicken sandwiches, why shouldn't the church use them to sell Jesus Christ?

One corporate value the church has been eager to adopt is the centrality of "the mission." It seems like any serious church these days must have its own short, pithy, and memorable mission statement, and ideally, it should be unavoidably visible—displayed in the church foyer, billboarded on the website, and perhaps even painted above the pulpit in the sanctuary. In my experience, churches are eager to out-mission each other. Everyone wants to be "missional," "mission-centric," or "mission-driven" these days. Years ago, while an editor at *Christianity Today*, I got an earful from a megachurch pastor when I failed to label his congregation as "missional" in an article. Failing to be missional is now an unpardonable sin.

And yet, the apostle Paul—perhaps the greatest missionary in history—did not see the mission as the foundation of the church. Instead, he understood Jesus Christ *Himself* to be the foundation. With his metaphor, Paul was echoing the words of Jesus from Matthew 18. When Peter correctly identified Him as the Messiah, the Son of God, Jesus affirmed him and said, "On this rock I will build my church." Scholars have debated the precise meaning of Jesus' words for centuries. Is the rock/foundation of the church Peter, whose name means "stone" or "rock," or is the rock Peter's declaration that Jesus is the Son of God? I suspect the ambiguity may have been intentional on Jesus' part. As the rest of the New Testament makes clear, Jesus Himself is the foundation of the church, which is built up through the testimony of those, like Peter, who proclaim Him to be the Son of God.

What is not ambiguous, however, is that what binds the true church together is not a task but a *person*. This is the radical meaning of Paul's metaphor. As we all, individually and together, draw into deep communion with Christ, we discover our unity and identity as His people—the new temple of God.

This is what the modern church's infatuation with business

strategies overlooks. Other organizations, including the most effective ones, are founded on some shared purpose—to sell a product, to make money, to elect a candidate, or to change a community. When the church copies their values, we can't help but make our mission foundational as well, and in a subtle twist of idolatry, the *work* of Jesus comes to replace the *person* of Jesus in our lives and in our churches. In the process, we cease to be a true temple of God and instead become just another organization with a product to sell.

 READ MORE: 1 Corinthians 3:5–19; Ephesians 2:13–22

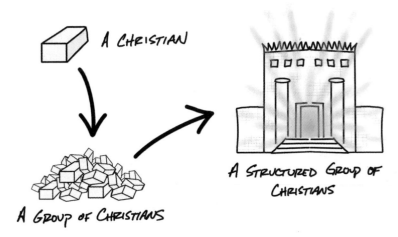

BRICK ≠ TEMPLE

A CHRISTIAN

A STRUCTURED GROUP OF CHRISTIANS

A GROUP OF CHRISTIANS

37 **IF JESUS WAS SERIOUS . . . THEN THE CHURCH'S MISSION REQUIRES THE CHURCH'S UNITY.**

THROUGHOUT 1 CORINTHIANS 3, Paul develops his metaphor of Christ's people being God's temple that is still under construction, but it's important to recognize that he uses this metaphor while addressing the problem of divisions within the church. He returns to this issue when he writes: "Do you not know that you are God's temple and that God's Spirit dwells in you? If anyone destroys God's temple, God will destroy him. For God's temple is holy, and you are that temple" (1 Cor. 3:16–17).

Paul's argument is as powerful as it is simple. Those who build God's temple faithfully will be rewarded (v. 14), those who build poorly will suffer loss (v. 15), and those who destroy God's temple will be destroyed (vv. 16–17). With this dire warning, Paul is speaking directly to those who are provoking divisions and factions among the Corinthian believers. Through their actions, they are scheming to dismantle the temple of God; to divide and destroy it. And those who destroy God's temple, God will destroy. It's the strongest warning Paul unleashes on the Corinthians anywhere in his letter.

The question to ask is: Why? Why is dividing the church such a grievous offense to God? Today, we take church divisions in stride. They happen all the time and for all sorts of reasons. Our flippancy about church divisions is due, in part, to our cultural captivity to individualism. We fail to see the collective church as critical to God's mission in the world. We think of mission as something undertaken by individuals, not whole communities. And, being far removed from the ancient world, we don't recognize the role of temples, which is central to Paul's argument.

Remember, in the Old Testament the temple was the centerpiece of God's mission and presence in the world. If the temple was destroyed, it was believed God's redemptive mission could not unfold. Without the temple, people could not rightly see, know, or encounter God. This is why, when the temple in Jerusalem was destroyed, it was utterly devastating to the Israelites. Their identity and purpose as God's people were bound to the temple.

This explains why Paul is so passionate about church

unity. Rather than a physical building, God's true temple is now the people of Jesus Christ bound to Him and each other in a community of love. At its core, church unity isn't about the blessings of harmony, and it's not simply a beneficial by-product of kind Christian people avoiding conflict. Unity is essential to the mission of God in the world. When the world sees formerly divided people who used to be filled with hatred, envy, anger, and rage, transformed and united into a people of love, goodness, and kindness—they will believe. When the world sees people once divided by race, color, class, and tradition, now embracing one another as brothers and sisters—they will believe.

But if church unity is lost, if the temple of God is divided, His mission will not be accomplished. As Jesus prayed before His death, we are called to be one so that the world may believe (John 17:21). Therefore, those within the church who are causing divisions are actually working to undermine the very mission and purpose of God. They are no different from the pagan armies that sought to desecrate and destroy the temple in Jerusalem, and whom the Lord judged harshly. This is the idea behind Paul's dramatic words of warning. We all know that divisions in the church are going to happen—just make sure they don't happen because of you.

 READ MORE: 1 Corinthians 3:5–19; John 17:14–23

CHURCH AS...

WINDOW or MIRROR

WE SEE CHRIST
AND HIS KINGDOM

WE SEE OURSELVES
AND THE WORLD'S KINGDOMS

38 IF JESUS WAS SERIOUS . . . THEN THE CHURCH SHOULD PREVIEW GOD'S KINGDOM, NOT PRESERVE EARTHLY ONES.

THE CHURCH IS INTENDED TO BE an outpost of God's kingdom. It offers a glimpse at the new world He is creating and the new society that has been inaugurated by Jesus through His death and resurrection. In His kingdom, the divisions of the world are transcended and previously separate people are woven together into a new household of faith. Simply put, the church is supposed to *preview* the new world God is creating, not *preserve* the one that is passing away.

Sadly, many churches get this mission perfectly backward. For example, in the American South before the Civil War, many white churches were established to reinforce the unjust structures of society rather than challenge them. Like everything else in the culture, whites controlled the church's leadership, the sermons, the music, and the prayers, while enslaved African Americans were segregated to the back of the church or the hot balcony. Everything about the experience communicated that people of color were inferior both in the world and in the eyes of God. More than 150 years removed from that evil system, we can clearly see the hypocrisy and wonder at the blatant disobedience to Christ evident in these churches. But had we lived in the pre–Civil War South, we, too, may have been blind to the problem.

Sadly, the church has often abandoned its calling to reflect God's kingdom in order to reflect the kingdoms of this world. In doing so, it worsens and solidifies the divisions of society rather than heals them. We even see this among the first generation of Christians in the New Testament. As we discovered earlier, the apostle Paul rebuked the church in Corinth for the way it segregated rich and poor Christians while celebrating the Lord's Supper. There's no evidence the Corinthians *deliberately* rejected God's command to honor the poor. They just didn't slow down and ask whether their cultural custom of economic segregation conformed to God's vision for the church. They uncritically allowed the currents of the culture to carry them along.

There may be churches today that are deliberately rejecting the call to reflect God's kingdom and consciously bowing to the values of consumerism, nationalism, or some other idolatrous kingdom of this world. But I suspect the more common error today is the same one made by the Corinthians. We simply don't slow down to examine our cultural values and habits and ask whether they are reinforcing the divisions of our society or healing them. We are the proverbial fish unaware of the water in which we swim. The problem is not that we hear God's call for the church and disobey it, but rather that we are so immersed in the ways of our culture that we do not hear His call at all.

To avoid this error we need to slow down, step back from our social assumptions, and reexamine them with the words of Christ and His apostles. The overwhelming message of the New Testament is that through Christ the divisions of the world have been overcome. The church is to be a new community, a healed society where the categories of rich/poor, male/female, slave/ free, Jew/Gentile, black/white, young/old, native/immigrant, liberal/conservative, and every other social division or hostility are mended. And any church designed—intentionally or not— to reinforce the divisions of society rather than heal them has betrayed the call of Christ. It has, like Judas, handed Him over to the powers of the world to be mocked and exploited for their own dark purposes.

 READ MORE: 1 Corinthians 11:17–34; Galatians 3:27–28

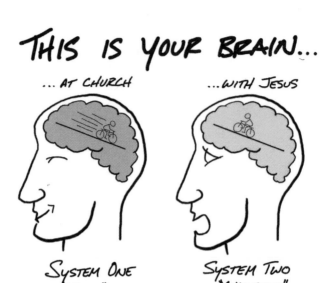

THIS IS YOUR BRAIN...

... AT CHURCH   ...WITH JESUS

SYSTEM ONE   SYSTEM TWO
"CHILL"   "CHALLENGE"

39 IF JESUS WAS SERIOUS . . . THEN THE CHURCH SHOULD BE CHALLENGING RATHER THAN COMFORTABLE.

IN OUR INCREASINGLY DIVIDED CULTURE, there is one thing that Americans still share in common—we all like to be comfortable. Our uncontested desire for comfort, however, has a dark side. Too much comfort is not only harmful, it can be downright dangerous. For example, a recent study by the Federal Aviation Administration found critical skills among pilots are becoming dull because they are under-challenged by a new generation of airplanes that virtually fly themselves. Ironically, the desire for safety through computer automation is leading to more accidents as pilots "abdicate too much responsibility to automated systems."[25]

I wonder if the same dynamic is disrupting the mission of the church? For decades, we have tried to make church gatherings a comfortable setting for both Christians and non-Christians to gather and hear Jesus' message. From the cushioned theater seats with built-in cup holders to the spoon-fed, three-point sermon with fill-in-the-blank pre-written notes—the only challenge most of us face on Sunday morning is actually getting our families to church. Once through the door, however, we can relax and switch on the autopilot.

Although the construction of comfortable church has been done to advance God's mission, like the airplane accidents caused by automated systems designed to improve safety, have our intentions backfired? Brain research shows that when a person is comfortable the more analytical functions of the brain required for learning shut off. Simply put, learning and transformation require discomfort—the very thing many churches work hard to remove from their gatherings. Psychologists refer to the brain as having a "system one" and a "system two." System one is the more intuitive "autopilot" of the brain that is engaged when relaxed, like when sitting in front of the TV or when listening to an entertaining, simple sermon in a theater seat at church on Sunday morning.

The other level of brain function, system two, is the analytical capacity of the mind that is necessary to examine assumptions, challenge beliefs, and assemble new behaviors and ideas. System two must be turned on, and the autopilot of system one turned off, in order to learn. The brain shifts gears from system one to system two when it is forced to work—when we are challenged, stretched, and made uncomfortable.

Jesus understood this. He expected His disciples to work in order to understand His teaching. He asked questions, wrapped His messages in opaque parables, and often taught in distracting settings. And for most of history, comfort was not the driving value in church architecture or worship design. There was hidden wisdom behind the hard pews, elaborate rituals, unique music, and liturgies that required kneeling, standing, walking an aisle, or making the sign of the cross. Many find these movements and symbols unfamiliar or uncomfortable. They were not part of a Christian's normal, everyday routine. But that was precisely the point. They shifted the brain into system two where engagement and formation occur.

I'm certainly not opposed to clear sermons or a safe Sunday morning environment, but our current cultural obsession with comfort in the church may have unintended side effects that disrupt our mission rather than advance it. If our goal is simply assembling a crowd or increasing the membership of our institution, then comfort should be our highest value. But if our mission is to make disciples of Jesus who obey all that He commanded, then we need to rethink our dedication to comfort. Followers of Jesus, like pilots, do not grow or thrive by being under-challenged, but by turning off the autopilot and being forced to take responsibility for their own life with God.

READ MORE: Matthew 13:10–17; Luke 18:31–34

DISCIPLES WHO MAKE...
DISCIPLES WHO MAKE...
DISCIPLES WHO MAKE...
DISCIPLES WHO MAKE...
DISCIPLES WHO MAKE...

WAIT, WHA[T]
A DISCIP[LE]

?

40 IF JESUS WAS SERIOUS . . . THEN A CHURCH MUST DEFINE A DISCIPLE BEFORE IT CAN MAKE THEM.

WHILE IN SEMINARY, I read a book about the church's mission with a pyramid-shaped diagram explaining the multiplication of disciples. It showed a single disciple of Jesus at the top connected by lines to three more disciples just below. They in turn each generated three more. The pyramid continued to expand down the page until hundreds of disciples occupied a single generation. The point of the diagram was to show the exponential impact of "disciples who make disciples." In the twenty years since graduating from seminary, I've seen some version of this diagram in dozens of churches and ministries, and I've spoken with countless pastors who believe in the mission of "disciples who make disciples, who make disciples." But it always provokes in me the same question: *What is a disciple?*

The multiplication diagram I first encountered in seminary is not limited to ministry. It's also popular in multilevel marketing businesses (MLMs). I'm sure you've encountered these through friends and family. They usually involve a gathering at home where someone pitches the benefits of vitamins, kitchen utensils, fragrant oils, or some other small, easily distributed product. The goal of most MLMs isn't merely to sell the products but to recruit more people under you to sell the products and receive a percentage of their revenues.

As those who participate in multilevel marketing businesses are quick to tell you, MLMs are *not* pyramid schemes. Pyramid schemes, which are illegal, also function by recruiting more people and redistributing money up the hierarchy. But according to the US Federal Trade Commission, the problem with illegal pyramid schemes, unlike legitimate MLMs, is that they don't actually sell a product. There are no vitamins, oils, knives, soaps, or office supplies. It's a pyramid without a product. This brings me back to the church.

At the end of Matthew's gospel, just before ascending back to His Father, Jesus commissioned His followers to "go and make disciples" (Matt. 28:19). Some have identified this verse as Jesus' marching orders for His church, and it's often cited

179

by church leaders as the biblical and theological justification for their goal of "making disciples, who make disciples, who make disciples." The problem occurs when a church or ministry can't actually define what a disciple is. At best they may define a disciple as someone who is plugged into the machinery of the ministry itself and therefore participating in its mission of making more disciples. But this is hardly a satisfying answer. It's like saying a widget is something that participates in making more widgets. It's a nonsensical, circular argument. It's a pyramid without a product. And like a pyramid scheme, any church whose mission is merely to grow and perpetuate itself will eventually collapse, but only after destroying the lives and faiths of many innocent people.

Unlike a pyramid scheme, the true church does not exist merely for its own advancement. It doesn't recruit new members, to recruit new members, to recruit new members. And Jesus' commission in Matthew 28 wasn't intended to be an empty circular argument. A disciple of Jesus Christ does more than make more disciples, and that something more is breathtaking in its scope and beauty.

 READ MORE: **Matthew 28:16–20; John 17:13–24**

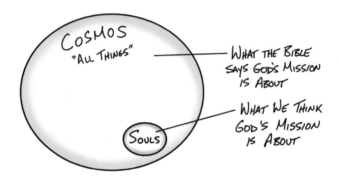

IN THE BEGINING GOD CREATED THE HEAVENS + EAR[TH]
... THEN HE RETIRED TO DO FULL-TIME MINISTRY.

COSMOS
"ALL THINGS"

— WHAT THE BIBLE
SAYS GOD'S MISSION
IS ABOUT

— WHAT WE THINK
GOD'S MISSION
IS ABOUT

SOULS

41 IF JESUS WAS SERIOUS . . . THEN HIS MISSION AND THE CHURCH'S ARE COSMIC IN SCOPE.

"I WANT WHAT BREAKS GOD'S HEART to break my heart." You may have heard this well-intentioned cliché in your church community. It's a sincere way of expressing a desire to be more like Christ, and that should be affirmed. But have you ever wondered, "What *doesn't* break God's heart?" Is there a degree of pain, suffering, or injustice that doesn't rise to our Lord's attention? Are there broken things in this world over which the Creator does *not* grieve? When we say certain things "break God's heart" we're implying there is also a category of things beyond His concern. That doesn't sound like the One Jesus said counts every hair on our head and notices every sparrow that falls to the ground (Matt. 10:29–30).

Still, the instinct to prioritize certain people, things, and activities over others is a part of every religion. It's a way of ordering the world into what matters and what does not, and then validating those who focus on the "right" things. It's why so many churches, whether explicitly or implicitly, function with a bifurcated and dis-integrated vision of the world. Most religious communities instinctually label certain things as "sacred" and therefore within the scope of God's concern, and a far larger group of things as "secular," which exist beyond God's care if not His sight. Sadly, this tendency has severely reduced our understanding of what Jesus accomplished on the cross, the scope of His redemption, and the breadth of the mission He's given to His church.

The New Testament repeatedly emphasizes the cosmic scale of Jesus' sacrifice. Paul said through the cross, God has "reconciled to himself *all things*, whether on earth or in heaven" (Col. 1:20, emphasis added). And in his most extensive articulation of the gospel (found in 1 Corinthians 15), Paul reiterates Jesus' intent to rule over "all things" no less than *eight times*! The cosmic scope of Paul's gospel fits with the Jewish vision of God he inherited from the Hebrew Scriptures that declare, "In the beginning, God created the heavens and the earth" (Gen. 1:1). The next verse does not say God then retired into full-time ministry.

And yet, that is how many churches function. We assume that God cares about redeeming souls but not bodies. We think

He wants a thriving church but cares nothing about a flourishing school. We believe God wants the gospel preached but is indifferent about whether a hospital is built. When the church narrowly defines "what breaks God's heart," it ends up producing narrow disciples who do not recognize the reign of Christ over every part of their lives and every atom of creation.

This error, according to Ed Stetzer, was on display on January 6, 2021, when thousands of rioters—many displaying Christian symbols—violently attacked the US Capitol. Writing about American evangelicalism's complicity in what unfolded, Stetzer, an evangelical pastor himself, said: "Committed to reaching the world, the evangelical movement has emphasized the evangelistic and pietistic elements of the mission. However, it has failed to connect this mission to justice and politics. The result of this discipleship failure has led us to a place where not only our people, but many of our leaders, were easily fooled and co-opted by a movement that ended with the storming of the U. S. capitol."[26]

In other words, the problem is not that the church failed to accomplish its mission, but that it too narrowly *defined* its mission. When huge parts of our lives and world are seen as beyond Christ's concern, we shouldn't be surprised to discover false gods defiling those domains.

 READ MORE: **1 Corinthians 15:20–28; Colossians 1:15–20**

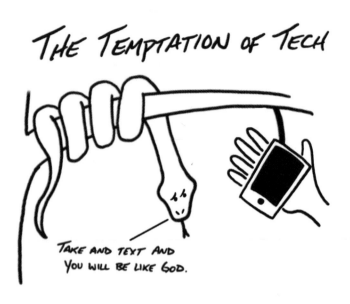

THE TEMPTATION OF TECH

TAKE AND TEXT AND
YOU WILL BE LIKE GOD.

42 **IF JESUS WAS SERIOUS . . .
THEN WE MUST RESIST THE
TEMPTATIONS OF TECHNOLOGY.**

THE APOSTLE PAUL SAYS Jesus "emptied himself" when
He took on flesh to dwell among us (Phil. 2:7). This means He
willingly surrendered some of His divine powers and qualities,
like omnipresence, in order to possess a physical body. For
example, the Bible tells us that God is spirit and unconfined
by time or space. "Where shall I flee from your presence?"
asked David (Ps. 139:7). When Jesus took on flesh, however, He
could not be everywhere, do everything, or engage everyone

simultaneously. He accepted the limitations of a body. To be incarnate is, by definition, limiting.

Technology, however, gives us the illusion of disembodiment and omnipresence. It allows us to escape the physical limitations of our bodies to transport ourselves elsewhere. In an instant, I can escape the reality of standing in line at the grocery store to text my brother in Los Angeles or distract myself with the highlights from Saturday's football game. Thanks to the seemingly omnipotent corporations in Silicon Valley, I am no longer limited by time and space. I can transcend my body, my thoughts, and the irritating people in my physical presence. Our phones have become genies that grant us godlike powers, but what are we losing in the process?

These divine-like temptations of tech are particularly strong within the church. Although the church is frequently referred to as "Christ's body" in the New Testament, the modern church would like to abandon the limitations that come with incarnate existence and embrace the divine power of technology. We have a God-given mission, church leaders say, so why not employ godlike technology to accomplish it? Advances in communication promise to help a church reach more people more quickly than we could ever do as a local, embodied community. The analog church of the past was slow. The gathering of actual bodies was messy and inefficient. The word was transmitted person to person, face to face. And care for souls required shepherds to be physically present with their sheep to listen, comfort, and pray. How old-fashioned.

With the arrival of digital, dis-incarnate ministry, which has only accelerated thanks to the COVID-19 pandemic, our mission can finally industrialize. Now every church can infinitely scale its outreach. The church can mass-produce disciples via YouTube, and tweets, and livestream its sermons to anonymous sheep anywhere in the world at any time. Dis-incarnate church is so much cleaner, more cost-effective, and massively more marketable.

The only thing inhibiting this more efficient kind of church is the stubborn fact that we remain embodied creatures. For example, a few years ago I preached a message about trusting God in our pain. After, I was approached by an older couple who had clearly struggled through the sermon. They were hanging on to each other as they came toward me—a detail I never would have noticed if I had preached via video. Speaking with the couple, I learned they had recently lost their adult son to a drug addiction. They had spent years trying to help him overcome his chemical dependency to opioids, they had prayed for his recovery with every ounce of strength a parent's love can muster, but he was gone. Their faith in God endured, they said, but it was weak and fragile. Their tears unleashed my own. I took their hands and together we prayed.

Standing with that broken couple, I realized evil makes no distinction between us and our bodies, and neither can the church's mission to overcome it. Jesus became fully human to redeem every part of us—mind, soul, and body. Any church that claims His name must do the same. Participating in the work of Jesus means accepting, and even embracing, our embodied limitations. It means assembling as physical creatures to care for one another as whole people, and not just as immaterial souls or online avatars. The grandiosity of our mission may tempt us to employ the tools of technology—and to be clear, they do have a role. But we must resist their idolatrous promise of effectiveness at the cost of our embodiedness. Christ's mission for the church does not require us to be everywhere, do everything, and engage everyone. Instead, the mission happens when we are fully present with the broken people right where we are.

 READ MORE: Luke 24:36–43; Acts 2:42–47

Assumption...

Reality...

KINGDOM OF GOD

YOU ARE HERE

YOU ARE HERE

43 IF JESUS WAS SERIOUS . . . THEN WE DON'T HAVE TO CHANGE OUR CIRCUMSTANCES TO CHANGE THE WORLD.

IN ORDER TO MEANINGFULLY PARTICIPATE in the church's mission, many Christians assume they are required to dramatically change their circumstances. For example, for those who say the church's mission is to "make disciples, who make disciples, who make disciples," the best, most devoted disciples of Jesus must be those who give their full energy to this work.

In other words—pastors and church leaders. To really engage in this mission, therefore, would require most of us who work outside the church to change our vocations.

From passages like 1 Corinthians 15 and Ephesians 4, we've already seen that the true scope of Christ's mission is far wider than most Christians have been led to think. Jesus isn't merely interested in saving souls or ruling over the church. He desires to reign over *all things*, which means being a disciple must extend to domains far beyond what we label "sacred" and far beyond the structures of the institutional church. But there's another implication of this wider vision of Christ's mission that we don't often acknowledge. If His goal encompasses all things, then fully participating in Christ's mission does not require us to change our circumstances.

Consider the apostle Paul. Some have called him the greatest missionary in world history; a man entirely devoted to the work of Christ and determined to "make disciples." And yet, unlike so many churches and Christian leaders today, Paul did not believe being a full disciple of Jesus meant changing a person's circumstances or vocation. For example, when asked whether a believer should change their relational status (married or single), their religious status (circumcised or uncircumcised), or their vocational status (slave or free), Paul gave a stunning answer: *remain right where you are with God* (see 1 Cor. 7:17–24).

Paul understood that the fullness of the Christian life was available to anyone, anywhere, because the fullness of the Christian life is Jesus Christ Himself, not our work for Him. And, in addition, he understood that God's mission to rule over all things meant manifesting His kingdom, as Jesus' disciple, right where we are. Paul's reluctance to remove believers from their existing relationships, vocations, and circumstances reveals how skewed our modern vision of the church, ministry, and mission has become. We assume fulfilling Christ's call means telling people to abandon their ordinary lives and activities to do more in the church, and we often define disciples as those who forsake earthly things to focus on heavenly things. But that's exactly backward. For Christ to rule over all things means welcoming the presence of heaven into the earthly things we are already doing.

Dallas Willard said it this way: "As Jesus' disciple, I am his apprentice in kingdom living. I am learning from him how to lead my life in the Kingdom of the Heavens as he would lead my life if he were I." Notice that Willard, like Paul, says nothing about changing his circumstances. Following Jesus doesn't mean becoming a Jewish rabbi. It doesn't mean becoming an itinerant preacher. It doesn't mean becoming a first-century carpenter. And it certainly doesn't mean doing more church work. Being a disciple who participates in God's mission means living your life, doing your work, engaging your relationships, and inhabiting your community *with Christ* and in a manner that manifests His rule right where you are.

 READ MORE: **1 Corinthians 7:17–24; Matthew 28:16–20**

PART 5

THE FAMILY SERVANTS

A dispute also arose among them as to which of them was considered to be greatest. Jesus said to them, "The kings of the Gentiles lord it over them; and those who exercise authority over them call themselves Benefactors. But you are not to be like that. Instead, the greatest among you should be like the youngest, and the one who rules like the one who serves. For who is greater, the one who is at the table or the one who serves? Is it not the one who is at the table? But I am among you as one who serves."

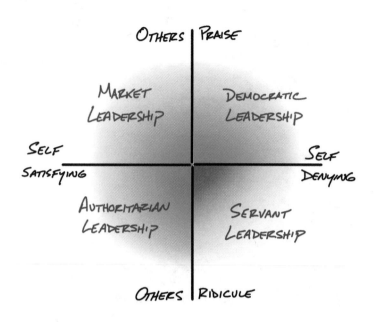

OTHERS | PRAISE

MARKET
LEADERSHIP

DEMOCRATIC
LEADERSHIP

SELF
SATISFYING

SELF
DENYING

AUTHORITARIAN
LEADERSHIP

SERVANT
LEADERSHIP

OTHERS | RIDICULE

44 IF JESUS WAS SERIOUS . . . THEN SERVANT LEADERSHIP ISN'T WHAT YOU THINK.

FOR ELEVEN YEARS I worked as an editor at *Christianity Today*. In the foyer of CT's office was a bronze sculpture of Jesus washing His disciples' feet. It was meant to remind us of our calling to be "servant leaders"—a phrase that's ubiquitous within the Christian subculture. The story of Jesus washing feet recorded in John 13 is often taught as a model of leadership. I've attended ministry conferences where the wisdom of "servant leadership" was unpacked, and the effectiveness of Jesus' humility displayed in John 13 was applied to the leadership challenges we face in the church. But is that why Jesus removed His clothes, put a towel around His waist, and washed dust and dung off His followers' feet? Was His intent to model a more effective leadership strategy to His apostles and us? Here's an unpopular thought—what if the scene in John 13 wasn't about leadership at all?

The context is important. Jesus and His followers had just arrived in Jerusalem where crowds had greeted Him with shouts of praise and an expectation of deliverance from their Roman overlords. Revolution was in the air and the disciples were inhaling it too. They fully expected Jesus to drive out the Romans, overthrow the corrupt Jewish authorities, and reign as the long-prophesied divine King over Israel. And, as His closest followers, they fully expected to share in His power and glory. The disciples even argued about who would get to sit on His right and left once His new government was established (see Mark 10:37).

But rather than ascending to the throne and taking political power, Jesus did the opposite. He descended to the lowest place by taking a towel and washing feet. It was a shocking and humiliating posture for any respectable rabbi or teacher, let alone the Messiah. But it's when Jesus came to wash Peter's feet that the scene really comes into focus. Peter said, "You shall never wash my feet" (John 13:8). To make sense of this you've got to understand the rabbi-disciple relationship in ancient Israel. It was a very common and powerful bond in which a disciple's identity was defined by who his teacher was. By leaving his fishing business and following Jesus, Peter was declaring, "From now on I am linking my identity with rabbi Jesus. From now on, what the world thinks of Him is what they'll think of me."

So far, that seemed like a really good trade. Jesus had performed miracles, was adored by the crowds—He'd even raised the dead. Peter's honor and identity were inexorably linked to the most powerful man in Israel. But then, Peter watched in horror as his Master stripped naked, put on a towel like a slave, and washed feet. Suddenly, his decision to leave his fishing business didn't look so smart. *If my Master takes the lowest, most shameful position in society*, Peter must have thought, *what does that say about me?* At that moment Jesus wasn't just humiliating Himself, He was humiliating Peter. He was deconstructing Peter's pride, destroying his honor, and exposing Peter's unholy ambition. That's why Peter refused to let Jesus wash his feet. He wasn't trying to protect Jesus' honor, but his own.

Once we recognize the story is primarily about honor and identity rather than service or leadership, it changes the way we apply it in our churches. A pastor who serves like Jesus isn't merely the one who's willing to do menial tasks. Shoveling snow off the sidewalk or emptying the trash in the nursery may feel like the ecclesiastical equivalent of first-century foot washing, but that's not really the point of John 13. Today a pastor may actually be praised and affirmed for performing those tasks. "Look at Pastor Steve taking out the garbage. He's such a servant leader." In our culture, there is honor in being a leader who participates in ordinary activities. But no one was honoring Jesus for washing feet two thousand years ago. If anything, they were snickering and mocking Him—foreshadowing the public humiliation He'd experience the following day on the cross.

Applying John 13 isn't about church leaders accepting menial tasks, but about church leaders accepting ridicule and embarrassment, about not being respected in society, and not needing the affirmation of their peers. It's having their ambitions exposed and extinguished. It's abandoning their desire for a bigger audience, larger platform, or more influence. Simply put, John 13 is inviting church leaders to crucify their own desires so they may be set free to truly love like Jesus. By washing His disciples' feet, Jesus was *not* showing us a more effective way to lead others. He was showing us what it really means to die to ourselves.

 READ MORE: Mark 10:35–45; John 13:1–17

ZOOM IN

I MADE IT!

ZOOM OUT

45   IF JESUS WAS SERIOUS . . . THEN WE SHOULD HONOR CHURCH LEADERS FOR OUR SAKE, NOT JUST THEIRS.

ALTHOUGH JESUS FREQUENTLY CRITICIZED and confronted the religious leaders for their hypocrisy, it would be wrong to think He did not value their role among God's people. In fact, on numerous occasions Jesus instructed others to submit themselves to the priests and other officials (see Luke 17:14). In other words, Jesus affirmed godly authority, even as

He denounced corrupt religious leaders. Likewise, throughout his letters to the churches, the apostle Paul repeatedly calls on believers to honor their leaders. Those who occupy these roles in the church faithfully and in a manner that emulates the character of Christ, he says, should be "considered worthy of double honor" (1 Tim. 5:17). But honoring leaders goes beyond those with titles like pastor, elder, or deacon. Paul says we should also respect those who introduced us to faith and who are ahead of us on the journey with Christ. We are to honor our *spiritual* fathers and mothers.

I sometimes struggle with these instructions laced throughout the New Testament. No doubt this is partly attributed to the great distance between that culture and our own. The ancient Near East was an honor-based society where respect and deference to elders and leaders was largely unquestioned. In his command to honor leaders, Paul was simply asking Christians to do what their culture already affirmed. (Although the reason for honoring leaders—their faithfulness to Christ and reflection of His character—was certainly countercultural.) Contemporary American culture is dramatically different. Our emphasis on equality and autonomy has made us skeptical of those with power, and our inclination is often to knock those in authority down a peg or two.

But I suspect my struggle with Jesus' command to honor leaders runs deeper. It's a sign of just how much I've been shaped by the cynicism and distrust of leadership that fills our society. We've seen so many people in positions of power—both inside and certainly outside the church—abuse their authority. We've seen so many hurt by their leadership and burdened by the dehumanizing systems they've overseen, often for personal gain. As a result, rather than affirming or honoring those who seek authority in the church, my instinct is to question their motives for wanting it in the first place.

To move beyond this cynicism, it's helpful to recognize the underlying assumptions of Paul's instruction to honor church leaders. The most common metaphor used throughout the New Testament for the church is a household. We see this even in Paul's instructions about selecting leaders for the church. They should manage their own households well if they are to oversee the household of faith (1 Tim. 3:5). Paul believes that through Christ we are brothers and sisters, fathers and mothers. It makes perfect sense, therefore, for Paul to draw from his Jewish heritage and reapply the fifth commandment, "Honor your father and mother" (Ex. 20:12), to the new family of God redeemed by Christ. Within the household of faith, we are to honor our leaders as our spiritual mothers and fathers.

Like the original command in the Old Testament, Paul's reapplication of it to the church emphasizes that we are contingent creatures. Both our physical and spiritual lives are dependent on others. Just as we only exist because of our biological mother and father who birthed and nurtured us, so our faith was born and nurtured by our spiritual mothers and fathers. The fifth commandment to honor our parents, and the instruction to honor church leaders, reminds us of our frailty and contingency—that we cannot obtain the most valuable things in the world without the help of others. These commands confront and unmake our illusion of autonomy and independence. The truth, which both my culture and my sinful pride want me to ignore, is that I desperately need others to lead me closer to Christ. The call to honor church leaders, therefore, isn't about inflating their pride, but diminishing my own.

 READ MORE: Hebrews 13:7–17; 1 Timothy 5:17–20

PASTORAL PEDESTAL CHECKLIST
DOES YOUR PASTOR...

- [ ] HAVE AN ENTOURAGE
- [ ] AVOID ACCOUNTABILITY
- [ ] REJECT NEGATIVE INPUT
- [ ] NOT EMPOWER OTHERS
- [ ] EXPECT SPECIAL TREATMENT
- [ ] NOT SHARE THE PULPIT

- [ ] LACK PEER RELATIONSHIPS
- [ ] HAVE A SHORT TEMPER

SCORING	
0:	LOW RISK
1-2:	MEDIUM RISK
3-4:	HIGH RISK
5+:	TAKE COVER

46 IF JESUS WAS SERIOUS . . . THEN WE SHOULD NOT MAKE PASTORS INTO CELEBRITIES.

WHEN PAUL AND BARNABAS arrived in Lystra they were celebrated as gods. Because of their powerful preaching and miraculous healings, the people declared, "The gods have come down to us in the likeness of men!" (Acts 14:11). Paul and Barnabas were called Hermes and Zeus, and the crowds prepared sacrifices in their honor. Of course, the apostles were horrified by this. They had come to proclaim Jesus Christ as Lord, not themselves, and they certainly did not affirm the pagan identities thrust upon them. When the apostles refused the people's worship, however, the crowds quickly turned. Their praise shifted to punishment as they stoned Paul and left him for dead outside the city.

I've visited some churches where I've wondered who is really the object of devotion—Jesus Christ or the pastor? Scripture tells us to honor leaders in the church because they teach us about Christ by their words and example, but in some places this is taken to extremes as pastors, and sometimes their families, are placed on a pedestal. When this happens, the pastor ceases to be a shepherd and becomes a sacramental celebrity—a personality on a stage or screen that functions as a singular conduit of God's grace. Ever since Mount Sinai, it has been the tendency of God's people to replace our invisible Lord with a visible idol. Today, we are not tempted to worship a golden calf, but a pastor with a golden tongue. Some Christians simply cannot imagine their faith without their favorite leaders standing in the gap between themselves and Christ.

Unlike Paul and Barnabas who refused to become objects of devotion, when a pastor lacks maturity or is haunted by insecurities, this exaltation can be intoxicating, impossible to resist, and ultimately very damaging to both the leader's soul and the church's health. With sad predictability, we hear reports of pastors tumbling from their pedestals. These stories are often accompanied by quotes from stunned church members naively unaware of how the pedestals *they* constructed contributed to their pastor's inevitable fall.

To be fair, not every pastor who falls slipped off their pedestals; some are pushed. If we have foolishly relied on them as our primary connection with God, then when our leaders disappoint us, and they all will, we are more likely to turn on them just as the crowd in Lystra turned on Paul and Barnabas. We will drag our fallen celebrity minister from their place of honor, punish them, and leave them for dead. The regularity of this should serve as a warning for any church leader desperate for approval and applause. Those who live by the crowd will also die by the crowd.

 READ MORE: 1 Corinthians 3:5–19; Acts 14:8–15

47

IF JESUS WAS SERIOUS . . . THEN AUTHORITY SHOULD COME FROM A LEADER'S CHARACTER, NOT THEIR POPULARITY.

It feels like a weekly occurrence—a popular pastor of another large church is dishonorably removed from ministry. Sadly, these stories about pastoral scandals are all too common and predictable. Also predictable is the outpouring of surprise and disappointment by the thousands who followed the leader's teaching and called him "pastor" despite most having never known or even met him. To many in his flock, he was a face on a jumbo screen or a tiny figure on a smoke- and light-filled stage. That may be part of the problem. Too many of us grant a leader authority in our lives and over our faith based on popularity alone, rather than through the personal knowledge gained by living in proximity with a leader where true character can be observed.

In a healthy church, real trust is not established via screens and stages. Consider how a healthy marriage works. A man and woman in proximity over time (dating) develop enough trust to then commit to a lifelong commitment of mutual submission (marriage). It's personal knowledge of the other's character that establishes the trust necessary for a healthy relationship. This is what Jesus meant when He told His disciples that false teachers would be known by their fruit (Matt. 7:15–20). The fruit Jesus intends isn't the size of the teacher's ministry or their popularity, but rather the fruit of their character. Likewise, Paul had character in mind when he told Timothy to select church leaders who are respected by all, and who have proven their faithfulness over time (1 Tim. 3:1–7). Authority is supposed to be predicated on personal knowledge of the character of those to whom we submit. But seeing their character requires close proximity.

When authority cannot be granted on the basis of proximity, however, our celebrity-obsessed culture will grant it on the basis of popularity alone. In these cases, we do not allow a leader authority based on a track record of faithfulness—because we don't actually know the person—but, instead, authority is granted based on the magnitude of the person's platform. I may not personally know Oprah, but surely millions of people can't be wrong. And I have no idea if Pastor Dave's character reflects Jesus, but look at how many people go to his church!

Sadly, as our culture's capacity to engage and maintain meaningful relationships deteriorates, we have seen a rise in popularity-based rather than proximity-based authority within the church as well. Just because someone has a large ministry or has sold millions of books doesn't mean we should automatically grant them authority over our life, faith, or community. As many entertainers, politicians, and church leaders have proven, it is possible to build a large platform and yet lack the character to faithfully handle it.

Our obsession with dynamic, effective celebrity pastors leads to a shallow authority based on the size of their platform rather than the gravity of their soul. Maybe we should reconsider the amount of spiritual authority we grant to people we do not, and cannot, know, and instead invest more energy into relationships with the godly women and men who are closest to us even if they are unknown to the wider world.

 READ MORE: **1 Timothy 3:1–7; 1 Samuel 16:1–13**

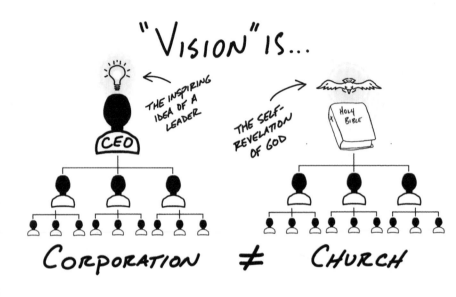

"VISION" IS...

THE INSPIRING IDEA OF A LEADER

THE SELF-REVELATION OF GOD

HOLY BIBLE

CEO

CORPORATION ≠ CHURCH

48 · IF JESUS WAS SERIOUS . . . THEN WE SHOULD BE SUSPICIOUS OF "VISIONARY" LEADERSHIP.

WHAT BINDS A CHURCH TOGETHER? In my years of visiting congregations, interviewing church leaders, and attending ministry conferences, one of the most common answers I heard was "vision." The belief that a church must have a compelling vision is now so accepted and ubiquitous in American Christianity that it's questioned less than most matters of doctrine or theology. I suspect that's the result of business practices deeply influencing pastors since at least the 1980s. I cannot remember the last time the value of a corporate vision was challenged at a ministry conference or denominational meeting. It would probably be met with laughter—like questioning the value of oxygen.

The importance of "vision" is often reinforced with a carefully plucked Bible verse or two. Proverbs 29:18 is a favorite: "Where there is no vision, the people perish" (King James Version). Contemporary church leaders have interpreted this verse to mean that a community must have a shared sense of purpose, a common goal to draw people and align them. It's a very short step to then illustrate the power of such vision by citing a successful business or corporation. *If Starbucks has achieved so much with a clear vision, just imagine what the church can do!*

There are numerous problems with this approach, but the fundamental error is a misreading of Scripture. Our culture uses the word *vision* to mean an inspiring idea employed by a leader to motivate others to action. However, you won't find that definition of *vision* in the Bible. Better translations of Proverbs 29:18, for example, use the word *revelation* or the phrase *prophetic vision*. Both of these are better at conveying what Proverbs 29:18 is actually saying. *Vision* in Scripture doesn't mean a corporate goal or inspiring objective. It's not what a leader uses to motivate their followers. Instead, when the writers of the Bible spoke about *visions*, they meant a supernatural form of communication received by a prophet or apostle in a dream. Think of Daniel's vision of the statue with clay feet, Ezekiel's vision of a valley of dry bones, or the apostle John's vision of the New Jerusalem recorded in the final chapters of the New Testament.

With this understanding, we can see that Proverbs 29:18 isn't saying anything about effective leadership or goals at all. Instead, the verse is reminding us that without God's words and self-revelation His people would perish. The church needs to hear from God Himself through the Scriptures and the Spirit in order walk in His ways. Simply put, vision is about God revealing Himself to His people, it's not about a leader motivating people to accomplish a goal.

So, in contemporary churches when leaders talk about "vision" it's usually not the biblical kind but rather the business kind, but many of us never notice the subtle shift. We just assume that it's right and biblical to construct a Christian community around a gifted leader with a plan. We assume that's how Christ intended His people to operate, and that a church's faithfulness is measured by how effectively it accomplishes the leader's inspiring vision. Sadly, this model of the church probably has more in common with Apple or Nike than with the apostles or the New Testament.

Dietrich Bonhoeffer, the German pastor and theologian who opposed the Nazis, recognized the danger of adopting the world's understanding of vision. He wrote:

> *God hates visionary dreaming; it makes the dreamer proud and pretentious. The man who fashions a visionary ideal of community demands that it be realized by God, by others, and by himself. He enters the community of Christians with his demands, sets up his own law, and judges the brethren and God Himself accordingly. . . . He acts*

as if he is the creator of Christian community, as if his dream binds men together.[27]

This is the real danger of accepting the business world's definition of "vision" rather than the Bible's. It elevates pastors and church leaders to occupy a responsibility reserved for Jesus Christ alone. Rather than a leader and his vision, the church is to be bound together by Christ. He alone is what unites the church, and any leader seeking to replace Christ with themselves or their vision is not serving the church. They are hijacking it.

 READ MORE: Acts 2:14–21; Colossians 1:15–20

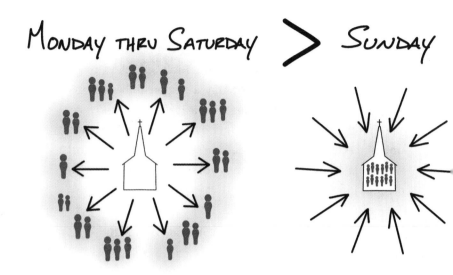

MONDAY THRU SATURDAY > SUNDAY

49 IF JESUS WAS SERIOUS . . . THEN CHURCH LEADERS MUST CARE ABOUT WHAT HAPPENS OUTSIDE THE CHURCH.

CHAPTER 4 OF PAUL'S LETTER to the Ephesians is essential if we are to correctly understand the role of leaders in the church. Paul begins by talking about both our unity and diversity as a Christian family. "But to each of us grace has been given as Christ apportioned it" (Eph. 4:7 NIV). He then quotes Psalm 68: "This is why it says: 'When he ascended on high, he took many captives and gave gifts to his people'" (Eph. 4:8 NIV). Here, Paul is referring to Jesus' victory through His resurrection and ascension by using familiar imagery of a victorious king returning from war. In the ancient world, a king shared the spoils of war by offering them as gifts to his people when he returned. But what are the "gifts" the victorious Jesus has given to His people in the church? We'll answer that in a moment.

First, Paul continues, "What does 'he ascended' mean except that he also descended to the lower, earthly regions? He who descended is the very one who ascended higher than all the heavens, in order to fill the whole universe" (Eph. 4:9–10 NIV). This is critical and often ignored in discussions of the church and God's mission. Paul says that Jesus came to earth (descended) and then returned to heaven (ascended) in order to "fill the whole universe." Simply put, the whole point of Jesus' mission—His birth, life, death, and resurrection—was so He could *rule over everything*.

Grasping the cosmic scale of Jesus' mission is critical if we are to understand what Paul says about the gifts He has given to the church. Paul writes, "So Christ himself gave the apostles, the prophets, the evangelists, the pastors and teachers" (Eph. 4:11 NIV). Paul says the gifts that Jesus, the conquering King, has given to the church are *leaders*, and their purpose is "to equip his people for the works of service" (Eph. 4:12 NIV). Some English translations say "for the works of ministry." And that has led to a lot of confusion.

Our culture generally uses the word *ministry* to mean religious activities or vocations. We assume pastors do ministry, but painters don't. We think missionaries do ministry, but manicurists don't. If a Christian organizes a Bible study, that's ministry, but when a Christian organizes a sci-fi book club, it's not. We define *ministry* as church work, and therefore we assume that Jesus has given leaders to the church in order to equip others to serve within the church as well. But that is *not* what Paul meant.

To truly understand Paul's intent, we must connect the giving of leaders to the church with the bigger, cosmic mission of Jesus to rule over the entire universe. In other words, we can't disconnect Ephesians 4:11 from the verse immediately before it. When read together, we see that leaders in the church aren't just supposed to equip us to do ministry within the church. Nor are Christians merely called to expand Christ's rule by growing the institution of the church.

Paul's concern is much, much wider. He's asking, *How does Jesus expand His rule over everything?* His answer: *By giving the church leaders, filled with His power, to equip His people to love and serve Him everywhere.* Not just inside a church building. Not merely through nonprofit ministries. Not only on Sundays. Therefore, if church leaders aren't helping you follow Christ faithfully in your vocation Monday through Saturday, or if they aren't equipping people to serve the community and world beyond the organized programs of the church, then they aren't truly fulfilling their purpose. They may be stewards of an institution, but they're not helping Jesus rule over the universe.

 READ MORE: Ephesians 4:1–16; Colossians 1:15–20

50 IF JESUS WAS SERIOUS . . . THEN CHURCH LEADERS EXIST TO EQUIP US, NOT TO USE US.

I FIND JESUS' PURPOSE for church leadership in Ephesians 4 to be beautiful and inspiring. It means pastors and Christian leaders are to help us grow into maturity so that our communion with God through Christ can transform our work, our relationships, our communities, and ultimately our world into one in which God "is over all and through all and in all" (Eph. 4:6). This dramatically changes how we measure a church leader's work. Ultimately it's not about how many people attend to hear a sermon on Sunday, or even how many volunteers are engaged in the church's programs. Instead, it's about whether people are deepening their life with God and manifesting Christ's kingdom everywhere they go Monday through Saturday.

Unfortunately, many churches don't carry this vision, and too many leaders narrowly define what it means to "equip the saints for works of ministry." That's why the vocations of God's people in business, government, the arts, education, the home, the social sector, and the media are so rarely acknowledged or affirmed within the church and why few non-clergy vocations are ever celebrated as genuine callings from God. Rather than *empowering* people to manifest God's reign in the world, too many churches seek to *use* people to advance the goals of the institutional church. Success is assumed when a person is plugged into the apparatus of the church institution rather than released to serve God's people and their neighbors out in the world.

I call such ministries "vampire churches" because they suck the life out of you. They view people as resources to be used rather than as God's saints to be empowered, and the wide acceptance of this posture explains, in part, why so many committed Christians are becoming church dropouts—or what sociologist Josh Packard calls "church refugees." In his book by that title, coauthored with Ashleigh Hope, Packard interviewed hundreds of Christians who've given up on institutional churches. Remarkably, he discovered those most likely to leave the church were also the most spiritually mature and often had years of deep church involvement.

A recurring theme in Packard and Hope's interviews is how dehumanizing the church structures can become. Sophia, a professor, said, "I felt that really all I was doing was functioning as part of a machine, doing what the machine likes, which is money and head count. . . . Nobody was mean to me; nobody did anything. It was like once you became a member, it was all about what you could do for the church to keep the church going."[28] Another church refugee put it more bluntly "The machine just eats you up."[29]

So, how do you know if you're part of a vampire church? Here's what I do—engage and get to know the people at the center of the community, those who are giving the most time to the institution—the pastors, elders, staff members, and volunteer leaders. What fruit do their lives display? If you generally find healthy women and men of peace, harmony, gentleness, and joy, it's usually a good sign. If those at the center are consistently burned out, exhausted, anxious, bitter, and unable to keep their core relationships healthy—be careful. Remember, the reason vampires want to suck the life out of you is because it's already been sucked out of them.

 READ MORE: Ephesians 4:1–16; 1 Timothy 3:1–7

APPEARS... STRONG WEAK

REALITY... FRAGILE ANTI-FRAGILE

51 IF JESUS WAS SERIOUS . . . THEN THE CHURCH SHOULDN'T JUST BE STRONG, IT SHOULD BE ANTI-FRAGILE.

WRITER NASSIM NICHOLAS TALEB has contrasted two kinds of systems or organizations. Some may appear strong and powerful but in truth are dangerously fragile. These are organizations in which one small change could threaten the entire system. The biblical metaphor of a fragile system is Goliath, the giant Philistine warrior. First Samuel 17 describes Goliath, his armor, and his weapons in great detail, emphasizing his unparalleled size and strength. He appears to be the perfect Bronze Age war machine designed to destroy any other soldier. However, when confronted by an unexpected opponent, a young shepherd boy with a sling, Goliath's greatest asset—his size and strength—became his fatal weakness. The Philistine's massive forehead was an easy target, and just one stone from David's sling vanquished the giant.

We might assume that the opposite of a fragile system is a robust one; an organization that is designed to withstand any single threat. But Taleb disagrees and says that the best systems don't merely resist threats, but actually grow *stronger* when challenged. He calls these systems *anti-fragile*. Consider muscles. When put under stress, our muscles don't break, and they don't merely flex. Stress causes muscles to rebuild themselves to be stronger and therefore better prepared for the next challenge they face. Nature is full of examples of anti-fragility, from our immune systems to ecosystems. Maybe that's why Jesus so frequently compares God's kingdom to slow, but unstoppable natural phenomena. A tiny mustard seed that grows to become the largest tree, a small amount of yeast that transforms into a large lump of dough, a grain of wheat that is buried but yields a huge harvest.

I find Taleb's fragile/anti-fragile categories helpful for understanding the church and why so many Christians and church leaders today are afraid. I suspect that in many places we have created very fragile churches, and we know—although rarely admit—that even a small challenge could destroy them. Consider our fixation on megachurches over the last thirty years. I don't believe there is anything inherently wrong with megachurches, but have we been naive about their fragility? Like Goliath, their size and influence project an image of enduring strength, and yet a sad number of megachurches have been brought low in recent years by often small, foreseeable events. The retirement or transgression of a single leader, which is not uncommon among all churches, has a disproportionate impact on larger ministries. The bigger they are, as the saying goes, the harder they fall.

And this fragility is not limited to the large ministries. Some Christian leaders are deeply concerned that even a small cultural or legal change may topple their entire ministry. *What if the government revokes the tax-exemption of churches? What if youth sports take over Sunday morning? What if non-Christians get to pray before city council meetings?* The inherent fragility of our churches, ministries, and schools helps explain, at least in part, why so many Christians carry so much anxiety today, and why we're conditioned to see a threat behind every cultural or political change. It also reveals why some prefer to retreat into isolated enclaves. Like immunocompromised children, too many Christians seek safe bubbles where they won't encounter anything that might challenge their fragile faith.

Contrast this with the remarkably anti-fragile church we find in the New Testament. Rather than a fearful huddle of believers worried about what Herod, the Romans, or those pesky liberal Sadducees might do, the early Christians appeared to actually believe Jesus when He said the gates of hell, never mind the IRS, would not prevail against His church (Matt. 16:18). And when the church faced genuine persecution, as it did in Jerusalem following the martyrdoms of Stephen and James, rather than extinguishing its mission, the church only grew stronger and its mission only advanced faster. And even today, we see that where the church is growing most in the world is often where it is most challenged. The church of Jesus is without question the most anti-fragile system in world history.

The question for those of us in the West, and particularly in America, is this—Why have we chosen to construct such fragile church structures? Why do we build ministries that rely upon a single fallible leader, one dynamic speaker, or that require massive and unsustainable amounts of money? Our devotion to fragile systems means that as the pace of cultural, political, and technological change increases, so will the spirit of fear among Christians.

Like the Israelite army that quaked at the sight of Goliath, the American church may soon find itself paralyzed and impotent. That's when we might discover it's the churches we've dismissed as weak and insignificant—the small, decentralized, anti-fragile networks of disciples found throughout the rest of the world—that courageously step forward like David to lead us through the challenges of our time.

 READ MORE: 1 Samuel 17:40–50; Acts 8:1–4

Notes

1. Warren Bird and Scott Thumma, "Megachurch 2020: The Changing Reality in America's Largest Churches," Hartford Institute for Religion Research, https://faithcommunitiestoday.org/wp-content/uploads/2020/10/Megachurch-Survey-Report_HIRR_FACT-2020.pdf, 2.

2. Quoted in James Twitchell, *Shopping for God* (New York: Simon and Schuster, 2007), 20.

3. Dean Schamberger, "Americans: Overworked, Overstressed," ABC News, http://abcnews.go.com/US/story?id=93604&page=1.

4. Josh Packard and Ashleigh Hope, *Church Refugees: Sociologists Reveal Why People Are Done with Church but Not Their Faith* (Loveland, CO: Group, 2015).

5. Bob Smietana, "Most Worshipers OK with Segregated Sunday Morning," Lifeway Research, January 15, 2015, https://lifewayresearch.com/2015/01/15/most-worshipers-ok-with-segregated-sunday-morning/.

6. Martin Luther King Jr. made this statement on many occasions, but he was summarizing an idea first spoken by Theodore Parker, a nineteenth-century century minister and abolitionist. See Theodore Parker, *Ten Sermons of Religion* (Boston: Crosby, Nichols and Co., 1853), 84–85.

7. Eugene H. Peterson, *Run with the Horses: The Quest for Life at Its Best* (Downers Grove, IL: InterVarsity Press, 2009), 101.

8. Quoted in Shane Claiborne, Jonathan Wilson-Hartgrove, and Enuma Okoro, *Common Prayer: A Liturgy for Ordinary Radicals* (Grand Rapids, MI: Zondervan, 2010), 375.

9. Wolfhart Pannenberg, *Systematic Theology,* vol. 3, trans. Geoffrey W. Bromiley (Grand Rapids, MI: Eerdmans, 1998), 286.

10. Paul Louis Metzger, "Walls Do Talk," *Leadership Journal,* October 15, 2009.

11. Ibid.

12. Parker J. Palmer, *A Place Called Community* (Wallingford, PA: Pendle Hill Publications, 2013), ebook.

13. Paul F. Bradshaw, *Early Christian Worship: A Basic Introduction to Ideas and Practices* (Collegeville, MN: Liturgical Press, 1996), 45.

14. Andy Hall, "Fantasizing Lee as a Civil Rights Pioneer," *The Civil War Monitor*, July 23, 2012, https://www.civilwarmonitor.com/blog/fantasizing-lee-as-a-civil-rights-pioneer. The article quotes *Confederate Veteran* magazine (October 1905).

15. Ibid. A later, more widely circulated version of the story stated the black man *did* receive Communion, and that Lee joined him at the table as an act of unity and Christian brotherhood. This attempt at revisionist history ignores the fact that Lee himself called the man's act "provoking and irritating."

16. Henri J. M. Nouwen, *With Burning Hearts: A Meditation on the Eucharistic Life* (Maryknoll, NY: Orbis Books, 2002), 30.

17. Alec Guinness, *Blessings in Disguise* (London: Penguin, 1997), 44.

18. Ibid.

19. C. S. Lewis, The Chronicles of Narnia: *The Magician's Nephew* (New York: HarperCollins, 2001), 47.

20. Sally Morganthaler, quoted in Paul Basden, *Exploring the Worship Spectrum: 6 Views* (Grand Rapids, MI: Zondervan, 2010), 104.

21. Paul Vitello, "William Pogue, Astronaut Who Staged a Strike in Space, Dies at 84," *New York Times*, March 10, 2014, https://www.nytimes.com/2014/03/11/science/space/william-r-pogue-astronaut-who-flew-longest-skylab-mission-is-dead-at-84.html.

22. Sean Brennan, "Bills Receiver Steve Johnson Appears to Blame God in Tweet for Awful Dropped Pass Against Steelers," *NY Daily News*, November 29, 2010, https://www.nydailynews.com/sports/football/bills-receiver-steve-johnson-appears-blame-god-tweet-awful-dropped-pass-steelers-article-1.450613. Steve Johnson later backtracked his original statement by tweeting, "And No I Did Not Blame God People! Seriously??!? CMon! I Simply Cried Out And Asked Why? Jus Like yal did wen sumthin went wrong n ur life!" See Chris Trapasso, "Buffalo Bills: Steve Johnson Tweets About Game, Clears Air on God Tweet," www.Bleacher Report.com, November 29, 2010.

23. Mark Labberton, *The Dangerous Act of Worship: Living God's Call to Justice* (Downers Grove, IL: Intervarsity Press, 2007), 37–38.

24. John Paul Lederach, *The Moral Imagination: The Art and Soul of Building Peace* (New York: Oxford University Press, 2005), 156.

25. Kells Hetherington, "Automation in the Air Dulls Pilot Skills," *Daily Caller*, August 30, 2011, http://dailycaller.com/2011/08/30/automation-in-the-air-dulls-pilot-skill/.

26. Ed Stetzer, "Evangelicals Face a Reckoning: Donald Trump and the Future of Our Faith," *USA Today*, January 10, 2021, https://www.usatoday.com/story/opinion/2021/01/10/after-donald-trump-evangelical-christians-face-reckoning-column/6601393002/.

27. Dietrich Bonhoeffer, *Life Together* (San Francisco: HarperCollins, 1954), 27.

28. Josh Packard and Ashleigh Hope, *Church Refugees: Sociologists Reveal Why People Are Done with Church but Not Their Faith* (Loveland, CO: Group, 2015), 67.

29. Ibid.

If Jesus was serious...then why don't we take Him more seriously?

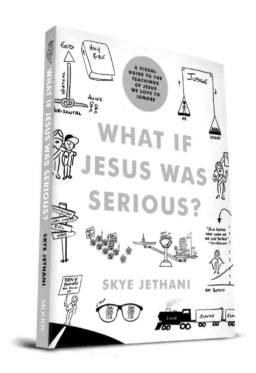

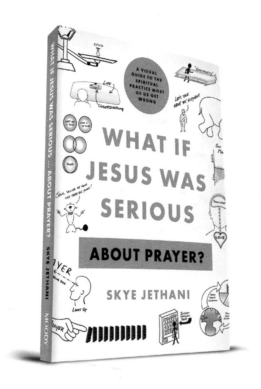

RETHINKING SUCCESS IN MINISTRY

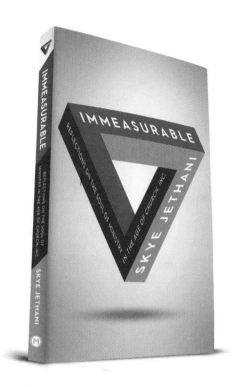

Immeasurable helps ministers recognize the cultural forces shaping their view of pastoral calling, then reimagine what faithful church leaders can look like in the twenty-first century. Through short essays and reflections on the pastor's soul and skills, *Immeasurable* commends the true work of ministry—shepherding, teaching, and encouraging—while redefining how we understand success in ministry.

978-0-8024-1619-3 | also available as eBook and audiobook